Health and Nutrition in Urban Bangladesh

DIRECTIONS IN DEVELOPMENT
Human Development

Health and Nutrition in Urban Bangladesh

Social Determinants and Health Sector Governance

Ramesh Govindaraj, Dhushyanth Raju, Federica Secci, Sadia Chowdhury, and Jean-Jacques Frere

WORLD BANK GROUP

ISBN (paper): 978-1-4648-1199-9
ISBN (electronic): 978-1-4648-1200-2
DOI: 10.1596/978-1-4648-1199-9

Cover photo: © Shehzad Noorani/World Bank. Further permission required for reuse.
Cover design: Debra Naylor, Naylor Design, Inc.

Library of Congress Cataloging-in-Publication Data has been requested.

Contents

Foreword		*ix*
Acknowledgments		*xi*
About the Authors		*xiii*
Executive Summary		*xv*
Abbreviations		*xxi*
Chapter 1	**Overview**	1
	Introduction	1
	Background	3
	Notes	17
	References	19
Chapter 2	**Analytical Approach**	23
	Quantitative Analysis of Social Determinants of Health and Nutrition in Bangladesh's Cities	23
	Qualitative Analysis of Urban Health Sector Governance	27
	Notes	30
	References	30
Chapter 3	**Findings on the Social Determinants of Health and Nutrition Status in Bangladesh's Cities**	33
	Child Health and Nutrition Outcomes	33
	Adult Health and Nutrition Outcomes	47
	Notes	57
	References	58
Chapter 4	**Findings on Urban Health Sector Governance in Bangladesh**	61
	Introduction	61
	Policy Makers: Coordination and Stewardship Challenges	61
	Health Service Providers and Financing: Fragmented Service Delivery	67

	Community: Gaps in Citizens' Health-Seeking	
	Behavior, User Satisfaction, and Voice	72
	Conclusion	79
	Annex 4A	79
	Notes	83
	References	83
Chapter 5	**Summary of Findings**	**85**
	Health and Nutrition Outcomes and Determinants	85
	Stewardship and Governance	86
	Service Delivery Organization	88
	Responsiveness and Accountability	89
	Note	90
	References	90
Chapter 6	**Looking to the Future**	**91**
	Policy Implications and Options	91
	Getting There from Here: Charting a Way Forward	95
	References	103

Box

| 4.1 | Primary Health Care Services for the Urban Population: | |
| | The Chittagong Model | 68 |

Figures

1.1	Conceptual Framework of Health Determinants	2
1.2	Distribution of Urban Populations and Areas in Bangladesh, by Administrative Division and District, 2011	4
1.3	Consumption Poverty Rates in Bangladesh, by Administrative Division and Urban versus Rural Areas, 2010	6
1.4	Distribution of Slum Settlements and Average Settlement Size in Bangladesh, by Administrative Division, 2014	7
1.5	Selected Urban Health and Nutrition Outcomes in Bangladesh Relative to Other Low- and Middle-Income Countries	8
1.6	Selected Urban Health and Nutrition Outcomes in Bangladesh Relative to Other Low- and Middle-Income Countries, by Poorest and Richest Wealth Quintile	10
1.7	Urban-Rural Differences in Selected Child Health and Nutrition Outcomes in Bangladesh, mid-1990s to 2014	13
1.8	Urban-Rural Differences in Selected Adult Health and Nutrition Outcomes in Bangladesh, by Gender, 2011	15
2.1	Health Governance Conceptual Framework	28

Tables

3.1 Average Under-Five Child HAZ and Stunting Rates in Bangladesh, by Location Type 34

3.2 Average Levels of Factors in Under-Five Child HAZ in City Corporations, by Neighborhood-Area Type, 2013 35

3.3 Effects on Under-Five Child HAZ in City Corporations, Base Set of Factors, 2013 36

3.4 Average Use of Maternal and Child Health Services in City Corporations, by Provider and Neighborhood-Area Type, 2013 39

3.5 Reported Reasons for Mother's Choice of Delivery Location in City Corporations, by Neighborhood-Area Type, 2013 40

3.6 Effects on Under-Five Child HAZ of Health Facility Use for Antenatal Care, Delivery, and Newborn Exam in City Corporations, by Neighborhood-Area Type, 2013 41

3.7 Average Levels of Health-Protective Household Amenities for Under-Five Children in City Corporations, by Neighborhood-Area Type, 2013 43

3.8 Effects of Health-Protective Household Amenities on Under-Five Child HAZ in City Corporations, by Neighborhood-Area Type, 2013 44

3.9 Average Levels for Mother's Migration to Current City Corporation for Under-Five Children in City Corporations, by Neighborhood-Area Type, 2013 46

3.10 Effects of Mother's Migration to Current City Corporation on Under-Five Child HAZ in City Corporations, by Neighborhood-Area Type, 2013 47

3.11 Average Levels of Women's Health and Nutrition Status in City Corporations, by Neighborhood-Area Type, 2006 48

3.12 Average Levels of Men's Health and Nutrition Status in City Corporations, by Neighborhood-Area Type, 2006 49

3.13 Correlates of Underweight, Overweight, and Mental Ill-Health Status in Women, City Corporations, 2006 50

3.14 Correlates of Underweight, Overweight, and Mental Ill-Health Status in Men, City Corporations, 2006 53

4.1 Comparison of Provisions and Implementation of Health-Related Mandates in Local Government Acts (Governing City Corporations and Paurashavas) in Bangladesh, 2009 63

4.2 Patient Perceptions of Health Facility Strengths and Weaknesses in Urban Bangladesh, by Type 73

4.3 Provisions and Observations of Citizen Charter for Medical College Hospitals Emergency Department 77

6.1 Summary of Key Issues and Policy Recommendations for Urban Health Service Delivery in Bangladesh 96

Foreword

Bangladesh has made remarkable progress on the health and nutrition-related Millennium Development Goals (MDGs), with major achievements in increasing immunization rates and reducing the rates of undernutrition, infant and under-five mortality, maternal mortality, and communicable diseases. Building on these successes, Bangladesh has now committed itself to achieving universal health coverage by 2032. Realizing this ambitious goal will require Bangladesh to intensify its efforts to address the unfinished agenda of communicable diseases and maternal and child health issues while also tackling newer health challenges, such as noncommunicable diseases, climate change, and urbanization.

Urbanization is occurring rapidly in Bangladesh, accompanied by the proliferation of slum settlements, whose residents have special health-related needs given the adverse social, economic, and public environmental conditions they face. Health and nutrition policies and programs over the past 45 years have focused largely on the provision of rural health services. Consequently, equitable access of urban populations—and the urban poor, in particular—to quality health and nutrition services has emerged as a major development issue. The knowledge base on urban health and nutrition in Bangladesh is also weak.

To address the knowledge gap, this report examines the health and nutrition challenges in urban Bangladesh—looking at socioeconomic determinants in general and at health-sector governance in particular. Using a mixed methods approach, the study identifies critical areas such as financing, regulation, service delivery, and public environmental health, among others that require policy attention. The report also proposes specific actions within and outside the health sector to address the issues, providing guidance on their sequencing and specific responsibilities of government agencies and other actors.

In sum, many of the substantial health-sector gains made by Bangladesh may well be compromised if urban health and nutrition challenges are not tackled. The same commitment that the country showed in realizing the MDGs is now needed to address the health and nutrition needs of urban populations. We hope that this report is valuable to policy makers and practitioners working on urban health and nutrition issues in Bangladesh, the South Asia region, and elsewhere, and can help inform the design and implementation of sound health policies and programs by our clients.

Qimiao Fan   Timothy G. Evans
Country Director   *Senior Director*
Bangladesh, Bhutan,   *Health, Nutrition, and Population*
* and Nepal*   * Global Practice*
The World Bank   *The World Bank*

Acknowledgments

This report was prepared by Ramesh Govindaraj, Dhushyanth Raju, Federica Secci, Sadia Chowdhury, and Jean-Jacques Frere, with substantive contributions by Kyoung Yang Kim, Quynh T. Nguyen, and Naihan Yang to the quantitative research and by Aniere E. Khan to the qualitative research.

The report team expresses its gratitude to several individuals and organizations for their support and guidance: the government of Bangladesh, mainly the Ministry of Health and Family Welfare and the Ministry of Local Government, Rural Development, and Cooperatives; the report's Advisory Panel, consisting of Alayne Adams, Patrick Mullen, Hossain Zillur Rahman, and Diana Silimperi; for feedback at the report's concept review stage, Judy Baker, Timothy Evans, Patrick Mullen, and Diana Silimperi; for feedback at the decision review stage, Anne Bakilana, Tania Dmytraczenko, Zahed Khan, Anna O'Donnell, and Vikram Rajan; for consultations, support, and feedback at various other points in the report preparation process, Shakil Ahmed, Bushra Binta Alam, Azam Ali, Nedim Jaganjac, Iffath Mahmud, Nkosinathi Mbuya, Abdu Muwonge, Monica Yanez Pagans, Muhammod Sabur, Owen Smith, Hyoung Gun Wang, Nobuo Yoshida, and Ming Zhang; for input to the concept note, David Wachira; and for administrative support, Shahadat Hossain Chowdhury, Ajay Ram Dass, Shabnam Sharmin, and Martha P. Vargas.

During the preparation of the report, the team met with various research and aid organizations, including the Asian Development Bank; the Bangladesh Rural Advancement Committee; the Embassy of Sweden; the European Union; the Japan International Cooperation Agency; the U.S. Agency for International Development (USAID); the U.K. Department for International Development (DFID); the World Health Organization; and the International Center for Diarrheal Disease Research, Bangladesh (ICDDR,B). The team received feedback from presentations at various conferences and seminars, including the 13th International Conference on Urban Health in April 2016; the Institute for Human Development, India–World Bank Global Conference on Prosperity, Equality, and Sustainability in May 2016; the Bangladesh Urban Poverty Conference in September 2016; and the Bangladesh Urban Health Policy Seminar in May 2017.

The 2006 and 2013 Bangladesh Urban Health Surveys were the data sources for the report's quantitative research. These surveys were administered by the

National Institute of Population Research and Training (NIPORT), MEASURE Evaluation (at the University of North Carolina at Chapel Hill), and ICDDR,B, with survey fieldwork conducted by Associates for Community and Population, Bangladesh, and funded by USAID and DFID. The report's qualitative research benefited from background studies prepared by Sabina Najme on regulations and by the team at Data International led by Najmul Hossain on community participation and accountability. The team is grateful to all the individuals who participated in personal interviews and focus group discussions.

World Bank management support for the report was provided by the Bangladesh Country Management Unit, primarily Tekabe Belay, Qimiao Fan, Sereen Juma, Rajshree S. Paralkar, Iffath Sharif, and Johannes Zutt, and from the Health, Population, and Nutrition Global Practice, primarily Rekha Menon and E. Gail Richardson. Funding from the World Bank and the Bangladesh Health Sector Development Program Multi Donor Trust Fund is gratefully acknowledged.

The team apologizes to any individuals or organizations inadvertently omitted from this list and expresses its gratitude to all who contributed to the report. The findings, interpretations, opinions, and conclusions expressed are entirely those of the authors, and do not necessarily represent the views of the World Bank, its executive directors, or the countries they represent. The authors are ultimately responsible for any errors or omissions in the report.

About the Authors

Ramesh Govindaraj is a lead specialist in the Health, Nutrition and Population Global Practice of the World Bank. He has almost 30 years of development experience in diverse settings, including as a practicing physician in India, in an international nongovernmental organization (NGO), in the research-based pharmaceutical industry, and as a senior researcher at Harvard University. He has published widely in peer-reviewed pharmaceuticals, health, and development journals as well as in edited volumes and holds adjunct appointments at leading U.S. universities. He is a doctor of medicine in ophthalmology from the University of Delhi and holds a master's degree in health policy and management as well as a doctorate in international health economics and policy from Harvard University.

Dhushyanth Raju is a lead economist, Office of the Chief Economist, South Asia Region, of the World Bank. He currently provides policy advice to client countries and conducts economic research on human development in South Asia. He holds a doctorate in economics from Cornell University.

Federica Secci is a health specialist in the Health, Nutrition and Population Global Practice of the World Bank. She joined the Bank as a Young Professional in 2013 and has supported operations and analytical work across different countries in Latin America, East Asia, and South Asia. She currently works on global programs, including the Primary Health Care Performance Initiative (PHCPI), for which she leads the country engagement work stream. Previously, she was a research fellow at Imperial College London, focusing on quality of care and behavior change. Her doctoral research was a comparative, qualitative analysis of the PHC reforms in Estonia and Lithuania, drawing from sociology and institutional theory. She holds undergraduate and master's degrees in economics and management of public administration and international institutions from Bocconi University.

Sadia Chowdhury is an independent expert on women and children's health and nutrition and health systems strengthening. She has extensive experience in health and nutrition program implementation with national and international NGOs, conducting research on program implementation and establishing midwifery and nursing programs in the private sector. At the World Bank, she worked in the South Asia, East Asia, and Africa Regions in support of health system strengthening and reproductive, maternal, newborn, and child health (RMNCH). She led the development of the Bank's Reproductive Health Action Plan (2010–15), oversaw analytical projects that drove innovations on both the supply and demand sides of health services; and researched fertility behavior in high-burden countries. She is a doctor of medicine from the University of Dhaka and holds a master's degree in public health from Harvard University.

Jean-Jacques Frere is a Global Health Fellow and serves as senior health governance adviser at the Asia Bureau of the U.S. Agency for International Development (USAID). Before this assignment, Frere worked for the World Bank, the United Nations, and in the private sector. He began his engagement in international health, humanitarian actions, and development activities by spending several years with the French charity group Médecins sans Frontières (MSF), of which he became the first medical director. He has extensive experience in fragile and conflict-affected states and is currently focusing on health systems, health policy reform, and urban health as well as various aspects of health sector governance. He is a doctor of medicine from Lille University (France) and holds a master's degree in public health from Tulane University.

Executive Summary

Introduction

In the wake of remarkable progress on the United Nations Millennium Development Goals related to health and nutrition, Bangladesh now seeks to achieve universal health coverage by 2032. To reach this ambitious goal, the country must radically intensify ongoing efforts to tackle communicable diseases and maternal and child health issues. At the same time, Bangladesh must address new health challenges arising from an increase in the rates of noncommunicable diseases as well as from climate change and urbanization.

Urbanization is occurring rapidly in Bangladesh. Although most of the population remains rural, 23 percent of people now live in urban areas (GOB 2014). From 2001 to 2011, the country's urban population expanded by 35 percent—an annualized growth rate of 3 percent. By 2050, the urban population is projected to account for more than half of Bangladesh's total population (UN DESA 2015). Slum settlements have proliferated as part of this trend, with a recent census counting approximately 14,000 slum settlements across the country (GOB 2015). Although these settlements differ in size, they share certain characteristics, including high population densities, a large share of migrants from rural areas, inferior public water and sanitation services, and poor-quality housing.

Despite increasing urbanization, health and nutrition policies in Bangladesh have continued to focus on rural delivery of health services and improvements in health and nutrition outcomes. The unique urban health governance structure in Bangladesh—which divides roles and responsibilities among the Ministry of Local Government, Rural Development and Co-operatives (MOLGRD&C), the Ministry of Health and Family Welfare (MOHFW), and urban governments—has further constrained the effective delivery of urban health services. Therefore, much remains to be accomplished in ensuring access to quality health services in urban areas, particularly for the poor. Significant knowledge gaps also persist regarding the financing, delivery, and regulation of urban health services. Even less well understood are the nonhealth-sector-related issues that have an important bearing on health and nutrition outcomes in urban areas.

The study uses a mixed methods approach to investigate the determinants of health outcomes in urban Bangladesh, underpinned by the World Health Organization's Commission on Social Determinants of Health (CSDH) framework (WHO 2008). The use of the CSDH framework enables a systematic exploration of both the social determinants of health inequalities ("structural" determinants) and the social determinants of health ("intermediary" determinants), of which the health system is but one. Within the CSDH framework, governance is an element of specific focus because the distribution of roles and responsibilities, as well as the relationships between urban health actors, are important in explaining health inequalities.

Accordingly, a quantitative analysis was conducted using community and household sample survey data from 2006 and 2013 to understand the extent and nature of variation in health and nutrition outcomes within and across city corporations (the largest cities) in Bangladesh—as well as which, how, and how much specific factors within and outside the health sector influence the variation in outcomes. The quantitative analysis seeks particularly to understand the variation in outcomes between slum and nonslum areas in city corporations.

A qualitative analysis was also conducted to understand the structure of institutional arrangements for urban health governance in Bangladesh. The analysis explores the de jure and de facto roles and responsibilities of, and relationships between, three key groups of actors—the government, service providers, and citizens—and the consequences of these roles and relationships for access, quality, and equity in health service delivery.

Findings

The study's key findings fall into several areas relating to urban health and nutrition in Bangladesh, as summarized below.

Urban health outcomes and determinants. Most of the average health and nutrition outcomes are poorer for slum residents than for nonslum residents. The exceptions are adult overweight, diabetes, and hypertension: averages for these outcomes are poorer for nonslum residents. Average socioeconomic characteristics also are generally poorer for slum residents than for nonslum residents. Factors such as age, education attainment, and household economic status are quite consistently associated with nutrition and health outcomes. Factors such as neighborhood environmental quality and health service availability by provider type are much less consistently associated with nutrition and health outcomes.

Urban health governance. Two important challenges pertaining to stewardship and planning are (a) a lack of meaningful coordination between MOHFW and MOLGRD&C on the provision of urban health services, and (b) the inability of the urban health system—particularly at the primary health service level—to keep pace with the rapid urbanization. These factors contribute to the inadequate numbers and poor quality of public health facilities.

Urban health financing. Urban governments do not have a separate budget allocation for health services or public health initiatives, and they have limited capacity to mobilize their own funds. Each urban local body may employ a small number of health staff, paying their salaries from its budget and through donor-funded projects. This is in line with the country's overall administrative structure, which is not fiscally decentralized and does not allow local participation in funding decisions. Urban governments also lack updated, standardized systems to determine who qualifies as poor and who should qualify for exemptions from user fees. Fees are not standardized across providers, nor are measures in place to ensure provider compliance.

Health-related regulation. Many regulations are weak and outdated, especially those related to government responsibilities and urban health service providers. For example, the law requires every health facility to obtain an operation license from regulators, to register with the urban government, and to renew its registration annually. However, regulators approach this process as a purely administrative exercise, with no quality controls in place. Monitoring and evaluation of facilities remains fragmented. Although the national Health Management Information System, under MOHFW, maintains data on ministry-run facilities, it does not do so for other public health facilities or for nongovernmental organization (NGO) or private health providers. This lack of comprehensive data makes it difficult to measure the performance of the entire urban health system.

Health service delivery. Bangladesh's health system consists of different legal entities, with limited horizontal and vertical integration and no mechanism in place to facilitate patient referrals. The health system puts inadequate emphasis on aspects such as equitable access to quality care, continuity of care, patient-centeredness, and patient rights. The sector also lacks a culture of accountability. Because of the strong focus on maternal and child health, services are not widely available for treating certain conditions (such as noncommunicable diseases) or patient groups (such as men), particularly among public and NGO health providers. Patients cannot easily access credible, relevant information on provider performance.

Overarching health policy framework. The urban health landscape is evolving in Bangladesh without a concurrent vision of how the health system should work in city corporations and municipalities. As such, there is a pressing need for policy makers to develop a comprehensive urban health policy in consultation with relevant stakeholders. The policy needs to better reflect changes in the operating environment, including increased rural-urban migration and shifts in the epidemiological and demographic profiles of urban areas. It should also consider the potential for multisectoral action to influence health and nutrition outcomes, the country's unique urban governance structures, and the needs of a working population. Any urban health policy should also recognize the proliferation of urban slum settlements and the special needs of their residents.

Recommendations

Based on the findings, the study makes several strategic recommendations to address the issues identified, strengthen urban health services, and help Bangladesh move toward realizing its universal health coverage aspirations.

Urban health governance. Establishing an effective governance framework for the urban health sector will require a multipronged strategy entailing the following:

- *Strengthening local involvement* to allow urban governments to take ownership of urban health services with financial and other support from the central government
- *Ensuring a cohesive partnership* among MOHFW, MOLGRD&C, other relevant ministries, and NGOs and the private sector by agreeing on a clear division of responsibilities, better coordination of financial resources and accountability, and stronger development of capacity
- *Aligning donor support* for urban health with the central government's urban health strategy

Urban health financing. To ensure sufficient, sustainable financing for urban governments to provide health services, potential options include the following:

- *Aligning financing with responsibilities for urban health* by (a) ensuring that the relevant central ministries allocate adequate funds to urban governments to provide health services, and (b) exploring ways to complement central government transfers with revenues collected at the local level
- *Updating and standardizing user fees* for essential services and the most common procedures
- *Standardizing methods to identify the poor and levels of exemption* from user fees, while ensuring full compliance among providers to honor such exemptions
- *Exploring the use of cash transfers to households*, with or without conditions related to health service use

Health-related regulation. To boost regulation of, and enforcement capacity for, urban health service delivery, Bangladesh should revise licensing and registration regulations and ensure rigorous quality control of public, NGO, and private health services. Professional associations can play a bigger role by promoting collaboration and fostering a stronger patient-centered focus among providers.

And the government should develop a comprehensive monitoring and evaluation system covering public, NGO, and private health providers in all urban areas, while also promoting evidence-based decision making.

Health service delivery. Bangladesh needs to restructure its urban health system to not only target specific diseases or population groups but also to address the needs of the entire population and foster a patient-centered approach. Such a restructuring will require urban health providers to move beyond maternal and child health services to also tackle noncommunicable diseases, reach underserved groups, and make services more accessible to the working population by expanding operating hours.

To those ends, promoting accountability and strengthening public trust in the system will require efforts targeting both supply and demand aspects. The government should expedite its plans to establish a functioning referral system to ensure that patients are properly assigned to specific providers. In addition, partnerships with the private sector have the potential to considerably expand the reach of urban health services. Private pharmacies are ubiquitous, while private clinics operate as the main providers of health services in urban areas, including to the poor. Partnerships with such entities could include experimentation with preventive and promotive health services as well as provision of a minimum level of quality care that is affordable to the poor.

Urban health policy. An urban health policy, within the broader context of urbanization and urban policy, should include a strong focus on the needs of slum residents. In the urban health policy, it is important to recognize that non-health determinants of health and nutrition outcomes (such as household income; mothers' education attainment; and water, sanitation, and hygiene infrastructure and services) are important to improving health. Thus, the policy should cover the roles and responsibilities of other health-sensitive ministries, including food, education, housing and public works, and water resources.

References

GOB (Government of Bangladesh). 2014. *Bangladesh Population & Housing Census 2011—National Report Volume-3: Urban Area Report.* Dhaka: Bangladesh Bureau of Statistics, Government of Bangladesh.

———. 2015. "Preliminary Report on the Census of Slum Areas and Floating Population 2014." Report, Bangladesh Bureau of Statistics, Government of Bangladesh, Dhaka.

UN DESA (United Nations Department of Economic and Social Affairs). 2015. *World Urbanization Prospects: The 2014 Revision.* New York: United Nations.

WHO (World Health Organization). 2008. *Closing the Gap in a Generation: Health Equity through Action on the Social Determinants of Health.* Final Report of the Commission on Social Determinants of Health. Geneva: WHO.

Abbreviations

ARI	acute respiratory infection
BRAC	Building Resources Across Communities
BUHS	Bangladesh Urban Health Survey
CHW	community health worker
CSDH	Commission on Social Determinants of Health (WHO)
DGHS	Directorate General of Health Services (MOHFW)
DHS	Demographic and Health Survey
EPI	Expanded Programme on Immunization (WHO)
FSM	fecal sludge management
HAZ	height-for-age z-score
LGD	Local Government Division (MOLGRD&C)
LMIC	low- and middle-income country
MDGs	Millennium Development Goals
MOHFW	Ministry of Health and Family Welfare
MOLGRD&C	Ministry of Local Government, Rural Development and Co-operatives
NGO	nongovernmental organization
RMNCH	reproductive, maternal, newborn, and child health
SD	standard deviations
UPHCSDP	Urban Primary Health Care Services Delivery Project
WHO	World Health Organization
Tk	Bangladesh taka
US$	United States dollars

CHAPTER 1

Overview

Introduction

In the wake of remarkable progress on the United Nations Millennium Development Goals related to health and nutrition—increasing child immunization, reducing malnutrition and communicable diseases, and lowering infant and maternal mortality—Bangladesh now seeks to achieve universal health coverage by 2032. To reach this ambitious goal, the country must radically intensify ongoing efforts to tackle communicable diseases and maternal and child health issues. At the same time, Bangladesh must address new health challenges arising from an increase in the rates of noncommunicable diseases as well as from climate change and urbanization.

Urbanization is occurring at a rapid pace in Bangladesh. While most of the population remains rural, 23 percent now live in urban areas. From 2001 to 2011, the country's urban population expanded by 35 percent, or by about 3 percent per year. By 2050, more than half of Bangladesh's total population is projected to be urban (UN DESA 2015). Accordingly, slum settlements have also proliferated: a recent census counted approximately 14,000 distinct slum settlements across the country (GOB 2015). These settlements vary in size but share certain characteristics, including high population densities, large proportions of migrants from rural areas, inferior public water and sanitation services, and poor-quality housing.

Until now, health and nutrition policies and programs in Bangladesh have focused largely on providing health services to rural areas. Consequently, urban populations, and especially the urban poor, have not enjoyed sufficient access to quality health and nutrition services. Knowledge about urban health and nutrition in Bangladesh also remains limited. Addressing this critical knowledge gap and the imbalance in policy and program focus will be priorities for Bangladesh if it is to successfully address the health needs of the urban poor and improve overall health and nutrition outcomes in urban areas.

Urban governments in Bangladesh are responsible for delivering public health services and preventive and curative care through public hospitals, clinics, and dispensaries, as well as for licensing private health providers. For these tasks, the Ministry of Local Government, Rural Development and Co-Operatives, through its Local Government Division (LGD), provides financial and human resources to help urban governments. The Ministry of Health and Family Welfare (MOHFW) is responsible for national health and family planning standards, strategy and policy development, and regulation as well as for secondary and tertiary care through its own public hospitals in urban areas (Adams, Islam, and Ahmed 2015; ICDDR,B 2015). This fragmented governance arrangement is an important constraint in efforts to improve health outcomes in urban areas.

To investigate the determinants of health and nutrition outcomes in urban Bangladesh, the study uses a mixed methods approach based on the World Health Organization's (WHO) Commission on Social Determinants of Health (CSDH) framework (figure 1.1). The use of the CSDH framework enables a systematic exploration of both the social determinants of health inequalities ("structural" determinants) and the social determinants of health ("intermediary" determinants), of which the health system is but one.

Furthermore, within the CSDH framework, governance is presented as an element of specific focus. The distribution of roles and responsibilities as well as the de jure and de facto relationships between groups of actors relevant to urban health (the government, service providers, and citizens)—all of which reflect broader sociocultural norms and values embedded in both social policies and social relationships—are important in explaining health inequalities.

Accordingly, a quantitative analysis was conducted using community and household sample survey data to understand the extent and nature of

Figure 1.1 Conceptual Framework of Health Determinants

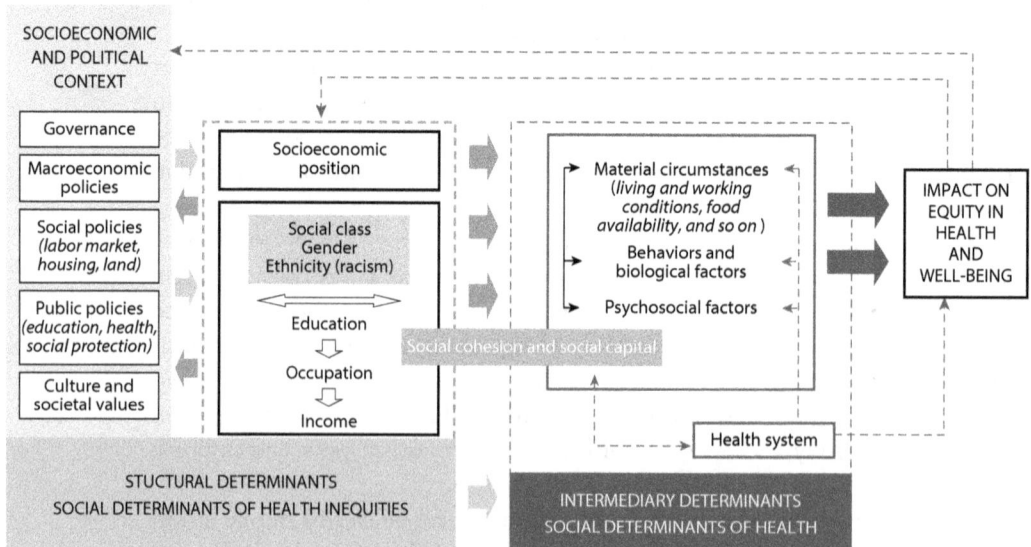

Source: WHO 2010, 6.

variation in health and nutrition outcomes within and across city corporations (the largest cities) in Bangladesh—as well as which, how, and how much specific determinants within and outside the health sector influence the variation in those outcomes. Of particular interest, the quantitative analysis seeks to explain the variation in outcomes between slum and nonslum areas in city corporations.

Governance is viewed as a critical determinant of urban health service performance in Bangladesh. To explore this dimension, a qualitative analysis was performed to understand how urban health sector governance in Bangladesh is structured and how this affects access, quality, and equity in health service delivery. Mixed methods are used because few rigorous and widely accepted quantitative measures of governance exist (Kaufmann, Kraay, and Mastruzzi 2007), and relevant, reliable data for Bangladesh are unavailable for such measures. A qualitative analysis also allows for a richer examination of urban health sector governance issues.

Background

To set the backdrop for the study, this section discusses three aspects:

- *Urbanization, urban poverty and inequality, and slum settlements:* urban share and urbanization rate, the types of urban centers, basic dimensions and characteristics of slum settlements, and the levels of urban poverty and inequality in Bangladesh
- *Urban health and nutrition outcomes:* health and nutrition outcomes in urban Bangladesh compared with those in (a) urban areas of other low- and middle-income countries (LMICs), and (b) rural Bangladesh
- *Urban health services:* The organization of urban health services, and available evidence on the quality of urban health services in Bangladesh

Urbanization, Urban Poverty and Inequality, and Slum Settlements
Urbanization
Classified as a lower-middle-income country,[1] Bangladesh is the eighth most populous country in the world, with an estimated population of 159 million in 2014 (World Bank 2016). As of the 2011 Bangladesh population and housing census, 23 percent of the country's population was urban (GOB 2014)—ranking in the middle of South Asian countries in terms of urban population share. In turn, South Asia's regionwide urban population share (28 percent) is the lowest among all regions in the world (Ellis and Roberts 2016).

In South Asian countries, including Bangladesh, official definitions of "urban" tend to relate to administrative boundaries. The extents of built-up areas often correspond poorly with the region's urban administrative boundaries. An alternative measure, the agglomeration index, is arguably comparable across countries and does not rely on administrative boundaries.[2] Using this index, Bangladesh's urban population share rises to 46 percent, while the corresponding share for

South Asia rises to 52 percent, ranking the region higher than East Asia and Pacific and Sub-Saharan Africa. By this index-based share, Bangladesh's urban population share continues to rank in the middle among South Asian countries (Ellis and Roberts 2016).

Establishing the urbanization rate in Bangladesh is complicated by a recent adjustment in the definition of an urban area. The 2011 population census introduced a stricter, administrative-based definition (GOB 2014).[3] If the older definition had been retained, the country's "urban" population would have increased from 13.5 million (15.5 percent of the total population) in 1981 to 42 million (28 percent of the total population) in 2011, an annualized urban population growth rate of 3.8 percent.[4] Under the new definition, Bangladesh's 2011 urban population instead totaled 35.1 million, or 23.4 percent of total population (GOB 2014). And the urban population growth rate was lower, averaging 3 percent per year from 2001 to 2011. These urbanization rates are roughly in line with the overall rate for least-developed countries over the past 40 years (UN DESA 2015).

Bangladesh's urban population is spatially concentrated. The country is organized into eight administrative divisions and, under them, 64 administrative districts. As of the 2011 census (when there were still only seven divisions),[5] Dhaka Division had an urban population of 16 million (46 percent of the country's urban population), Chittagong Division had 7 million people (21 percent), and the remaining divisions each had 1 to 3 million people (GOB 2014) (figure 1.2, panel a). At the district level, Dhaka District had an urban population of 9.3 million people (28 percent of the country's urban population), Chittagong District had 3.2 million people (9 percent), and each of the other districts had 100,000 to 1 million people (figure 1.2, panel b).

Figure 1.2 Distribution of Urban Populations and Areas in Bangladesh, by Administrative Division and District, 2011

a. Divisions

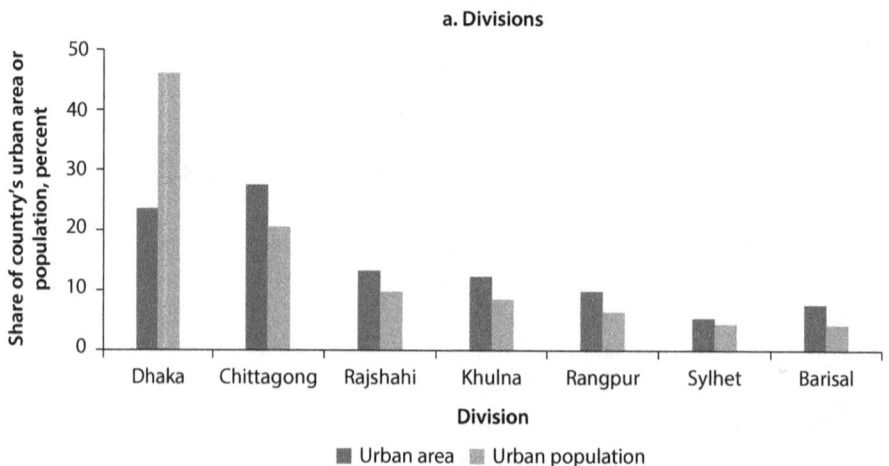

Urban area   Urban population

figure continues next page

Figure 1.2 Distribution of Urban Populations and Areas in Bangladesh, by Administrative Division and District, 2011 *(continued)*

b. Districts

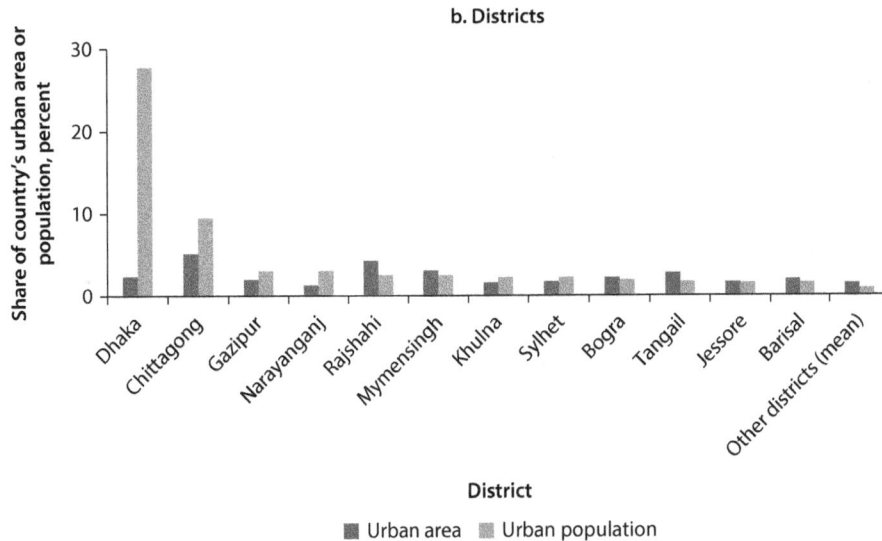

Source: Statistics from GOB 2014.

Urban centers in Bangladesh are organized into three geographically distinct levels, from larger to smaller population size: city corporations, municipal cities and towns (paurashavas), and upazilla headquarters. As of 2011, Bangladesh had 506 urban centers: six city corporations (Barisal, Chittagong, Dhaka, Khulna, Rajshahi, and Sylhet); 311 municipal cities and towns; and 189 upazilla headquarters (GOB 2014). The six city corporations accounted for 34 percent of the country's total urban population in 2011.

Since 2011, the number of urban centers has grown, and some have moved up in administrative level as well. The number of city corporations has grown from 6 to 11, with four newly incorporated city corporations: Comilla (in 2011), Gazipur (in 2013), Narayanganj (in 2011), and Rangpur (in 2012). Dhaka city corporation was bifurcated into Dhaka North and Dhaka South city corporations in 2011. Based on published census statistics (GOB 2014), the study estimates that these 11 city corporations accounted for 41 percent of the country's total urban population in 2011.

Urban Poverty and Inequality

It is well recognized that the distribution of economic welfare, measured by household consumption-based poverty and inequality, is associated with the distribution of individual health outcomes. Poverty and inequality statistics for Bangladesh are available at the national and division levels as well as within divisions by statistical metropolitan area (SMA), municipal cities and towns, and rural areas. The estimated consumption-based poverty rate in urban Bangladesh was 21 percent in 2010—higher than in all other South Asian countries except

Figure 1.3 Consumption Poverty Rates in Bangladesh, by Administrative Division and Urban versus Rural Areas, 2010

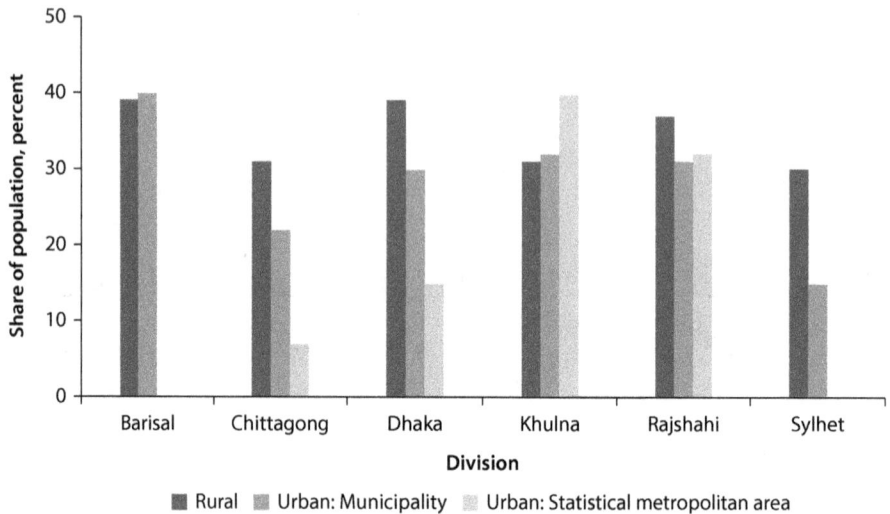

Source: Statistics from World Bank 2013, based on 2010 Bangladesh Household Income and Expenditure Survey (HIES).
Note: The 2010 Bangladesh HIES is representative for 16 strata: 6 urban, 6 rural, and 4 statistical metropolitan areas (GOB 2011). These strata are organized by administrative division in the figure. There were six divisions in existence when the 2010 HIES sample was drawn. Poverty rates are based on the 2005 national poverty line of Tk 861.6 (World Bank 2013).

Afghanistan (Ellis and Roberts 2016). The estimated poverty rate was lower in urban areas than in rural areas (21 percent versus 35 percent), as were the estimated depth and severity of poverty (World Bank 2013).[6]

The urban poverty rate varies across divisions, both in absolute terms and relative to the rural poverty rate (figure 1.3). Poverty rates in SMAs and municipal cities and towns are either similar to or higher than the rural poverty rates for Barisal, Khulna, and Rajshahi Divisions, whereas the reverse holds for Chittagong, Dhaka, and Sylhet Divisions. Poverty rates in SMAs and municipal cities and towns for Chittagong, Dhaka, and Sylhet Divisions tend to be lower than in corresponding areas for other divisions (World Bank 2013).

Over the 2000–10 period, the country's urban poverty rate fell from 35 percent to 21 percent (World Bank 2013). The rate of decline was comparable between urban and rural areas (where poverty rates declined from 52 percent to 35 percent over the same period). Estimated consumption-based inequality in 2010, measured by the Gini coefficient, was higher in urban areas than rural ones (0.33 versus 0.27).[7] Inequality declined since 2000 in urban areas (from 0.37 in 2000 to 0.33 in 2010), while it remained unchanged in rural areas (World Bank 2013).

Slum Settlements

A 2014 census of slum settlements enumerated approximately 14,000 distinct slum settlements across city corporations (65 percent), municipal cities and towns (24 percent), and upazilla headquarters and other urban areas

Figure 1.4 Distribution of Slum Settlements and Average Settlement Size in Bangladesh, by Administrative Division, 2014

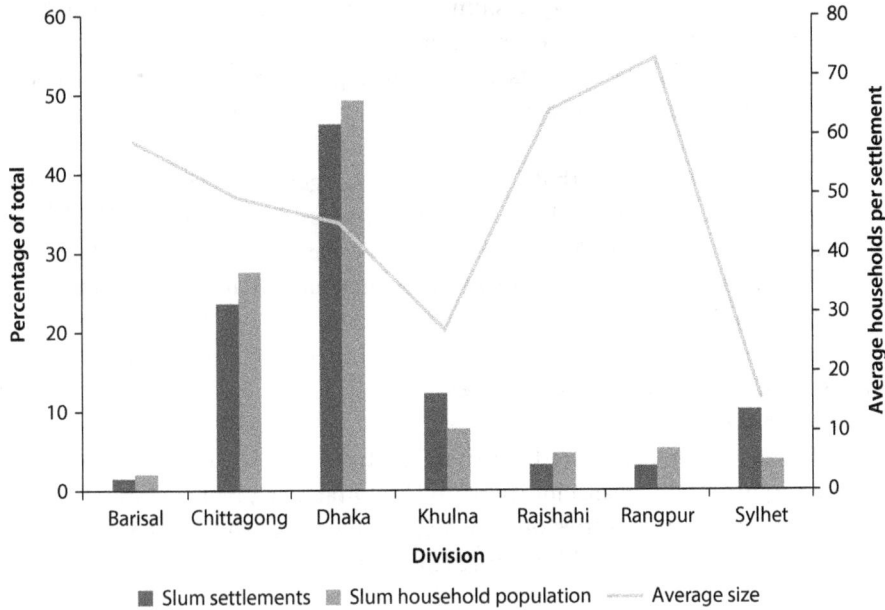

■ Slum settlements ■ Slum household population ----- Average size

Source: Statistics from GOB 2015.

(11 percent) (GOB 2015). Chittagong and Dhaka Divisions accounted for the largest shares of slum settlements (71 percent) and slum households (77 percent) (figure 1.4). Within these divisions, Chittagong, Dhaka North, Dhaka South, and Gazipur city corporations accounted for most of the slum settlements and population. The average size of slum settlements ranged from 15 households in Sylhet Division to 73 households in Rangpur Division; in the middle of the range was Dhaka Division (averaging 49 households) and Chittagong Division (45 households).

An independent census and mapping of slum settlements conducted about 10 years earlier, in 2005, had counted about 9,000 slum settlements in the six city corporations that existed at the time.[8] These city corporations had a total slum population of 5.4 million, or 35 percent of the overall slum population (Angeles and others 2009).[9]

The 2005 independent census had several interesting findings on the characteristics of slum settlements in Bangladesh, four of which are notable (Angeles and others 2009):

- Slum settlements within and across cities varied widely in terms of population size as well as housing and public environmental conditions. Large slum settlements were a feature of the larger cities.
- Waste management (garbage disposal and collection and sanitation) tended to be poorer than other public environmental facilities in slum settlements.

- The vast majority of slum settlements were situated on private lands, where slum residents tended to have secure tenure. In addition, housing construction tended to be of better quality in slum settlements on private lands, presumably a result of residents having secure tenure.
- A large share of slum residents were rural migrants, mostly from rural communities near the city corporation.

Case studies indicate that slum residents generally live under poor socioeconomic conditions (Hossain, Moniruzzaman, and Islam 2010; Islam, Farukuzzaman, and Islam 2014; Nahar and Rahman 2013). These findings are consistent with evidence for slum residents globally (Marx, Stoker, and Suri 2013; UN-Habitat 2016).

Urban Health and Nutrition Outcomes
International Comparison
Bangladesh's urban health and nutrition picture relative to other LMICs is mixed, varying by the health indicator. In WHO rankings, Bangladesh fares better than many other countries on urban infant mortality and adult female obesity, but worse on urban child stunting (figure 1.5).

Figure 1.5 Selected Urban Health and Nutrition Outcomes in Bangladesh Relative to Other Low- and Middle-Income Countries

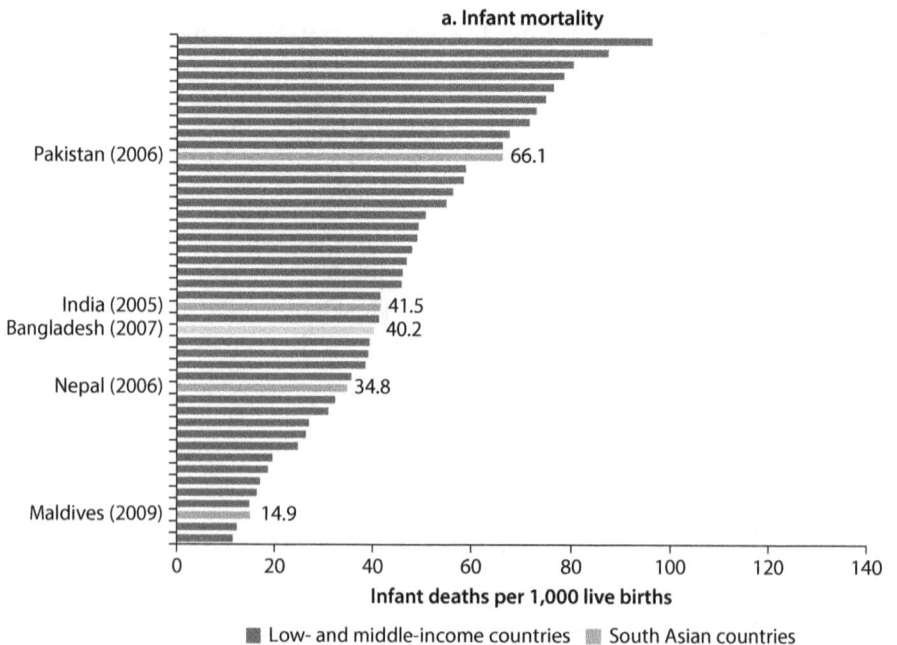

a. Infant mortality

Pakistan (2006) 66.1
India (2005) 41.5
Bangladesh (2007) 40.2
Nepal (2006) 34.8
Maldives (2009) 14.9

Infant deaths per 1,000 live births

■ Low- and middle-income countries ▨ South Asian countries

figure continues next page

Figure 1.5 Selected Urban Health and Nutrition Outcomes in Bangladesh Relative to Other Low- and Middle-Income Countries *(continued)*

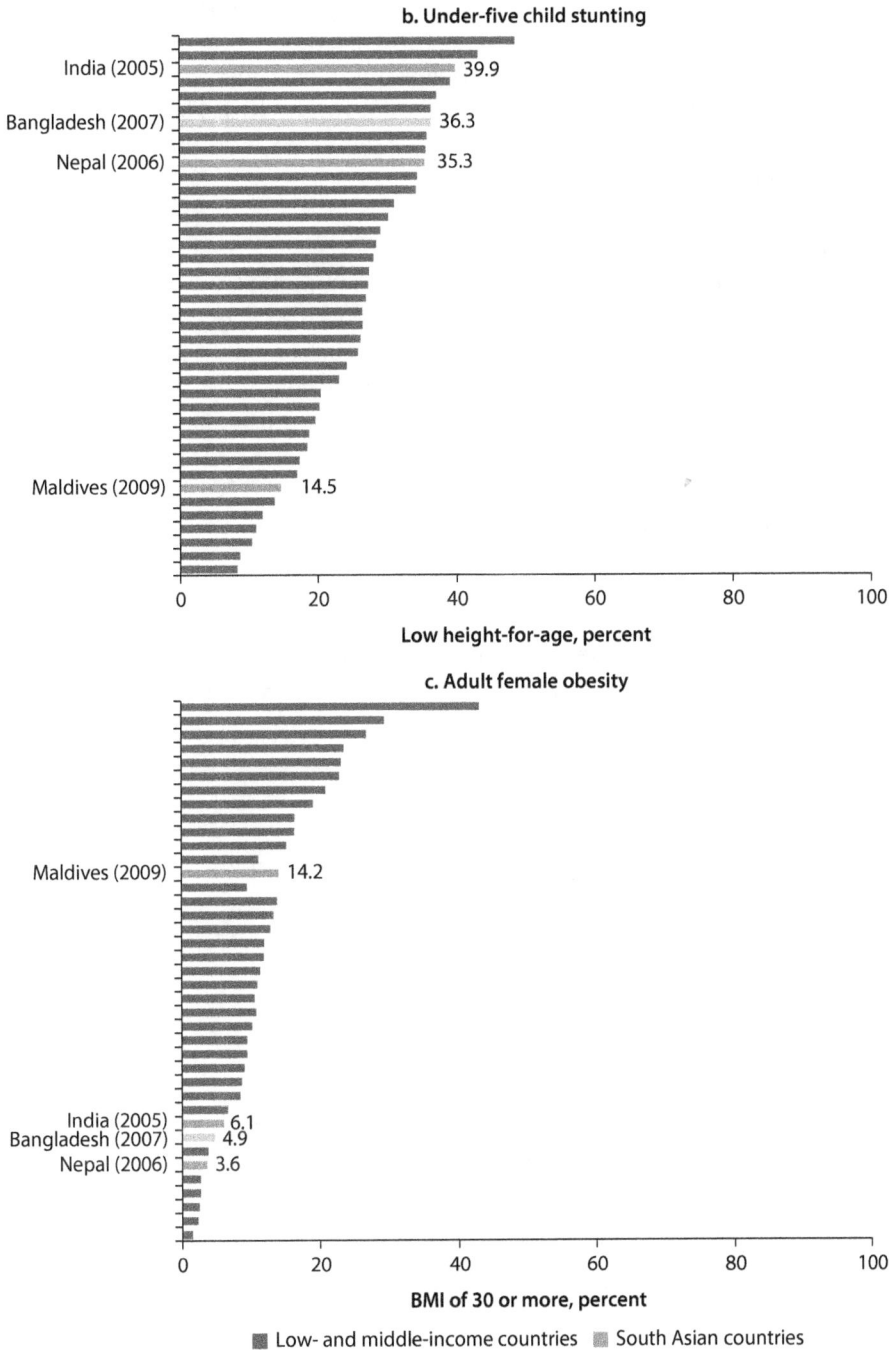

b. Under-five child stunting

India (2005) 39.9
Bangladesh (2007) 36.3
Nepal (2006) 35.3
Maldives (2009) 14.5

Low height-for-age, percent

c. Adult female obesity

Maldives (2009) 14.2
India (2005) 6.1
Bangladesh (2007) 4.9
Nepal (2006) 3.6

BMI of 30 or more, percent

▪ Low- and middle-income countries ▪ South Asian countries

Source: Statistics from the World Health Organization Global Health Observatory Data Repository (accessed March 13, 2016), http://apps.who.int/gho/data/node.home.
Note: Figure includes low- and middle-income countries having statistics for the indicators in the period 2005–09.
BMI = body mass index.

The country's relative status also depends on the urban subpopulation for the indicator, specifically whether the measure is for the poor or the rich. Bangladesh ranks worse than many other LMICs regarding urban infant mortality and child stunting among the poorest households (in the lowest wealth quintile). It also ranks worse than other countries on urban adult female obesity among the richest households (in the highest wealth quintile) (figure 1.6). These patterns are not unique to urban Bangladesh in South Asia; urban India and urban Nepal exhibit similar patterns.[10]

Urban-Rural Differences

Differences between urban and rural areas in average health and nutrition outcomes in Bangladesh are consistent with the patterns documented for LMICs in general (Van de Poel, O'Donnell, and Van Doorslaer 2007). For children, the rates of infant mortality, under-five stunting (low height-for-age), and under-five wasting (low weight-for-height) are lower in urban than in rural areas (figure 1.7). Based on visual inspection, trends over Bangladesh Demographic and Health Survey (DHS) rounds from the mid-1990s to 2014 do not indicate either marked convergence or divergence in these rates between urban and rural areas.

Figure 1.6 Selected Urban Health and Nutrition Outcomes in Bangladesh Relative to Other Low- and Middle-Income Countries, by Poorest and Richest Wealth Quintile

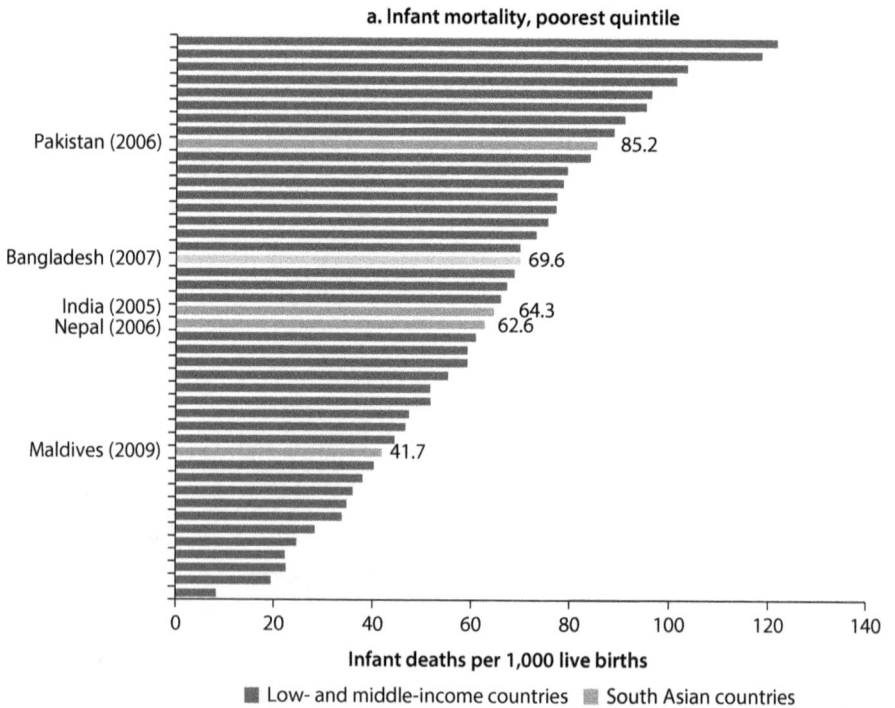

a. Infant mortality, poorest quintile

Pakistan (2006) — 85.2
Bangladesh (2007) — 69.6
India (2005) — 64.3
Nepal (2006) — 62.6
Maldives (2009) — 41.7

Infant deaths per 1,000 live births

■ Low- and middle-income countries   ■ South Asian countries

figure continues next page

Figure 1.6 Selected Urban Health and Nutrition Outcomes in Bangladesh Relative to Other Low- and Middle-Income Countries, by Poorest and Richest Wealth Quintile *(continued)*

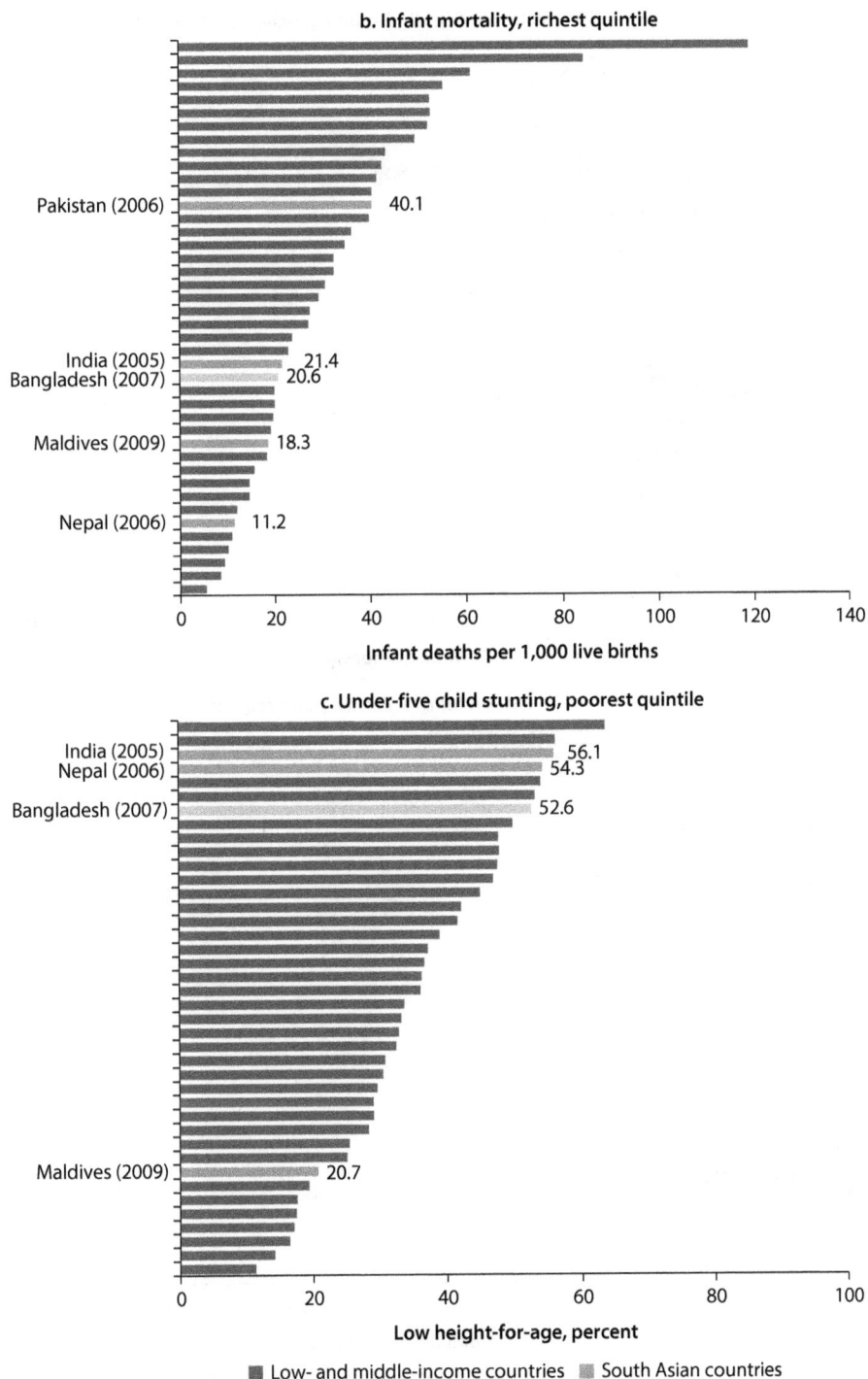

b. Infant mortality, richest quintile

Pakistan (2006) 40.1

India (2005) 21.4
Bangladesh (2007) 20.6

Maldives (2009) 18.3

Nepal (2006) 11.2

Infant deaths per 1,000 live births

c. Under-five child stunting, poorest quintile

India (2005) 56.1
Nepal (2006) 54.3

Bangladesh (2007) 52.6

Maldives (2009) 20.7

Low height-for-age, percent

■ Low- and middle-income countries ■ South Asian countries

figure continues next page

Health and Nutrition in Urban Bangladesh • http://dx.doi.org/10.1596/978-1-4648-1199-9

Figure 1.6 Selected Urban Health and Nutrition Outcomes in Bangladesh Relative to Other Low- and Middle-Income Countries, by Poorest and Richest Wealth Quintile *(continued)*

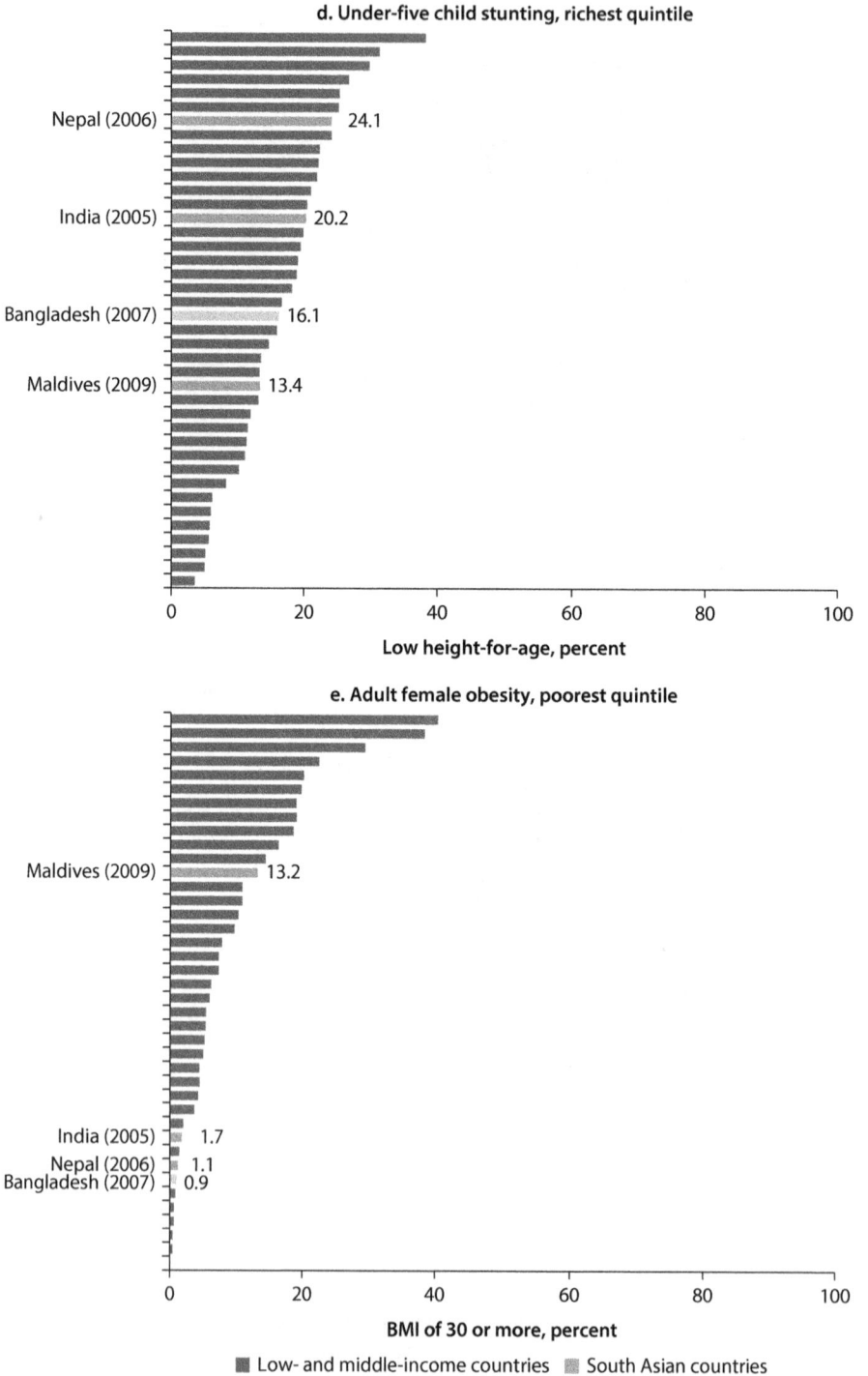

d. Under-five child stunting, richest quintile

Nepal (2006) 24.1
India (2005) 20.2
Bangladesh (2007) 16.1
Maldives (2009) 13.4

Low height-for-age, percent

e. Adult female obesity, poorest quintile

Maldives (2009) 13.2
India (2005) 1.7
Nepal (2006) 1.1
Bangladesh (2007) 0.9

BMI of 30 or more, percent

■ Low- and middle-income countries   ▨ South Asian countries

figure continues next page

Figure 1.6 Selected Urban Health and Nutrition Outcomes in Bangladesh Relative to Other Low- and Middle-Income Countries, by Poorest and Richest Wealth Quintile *(continued)*

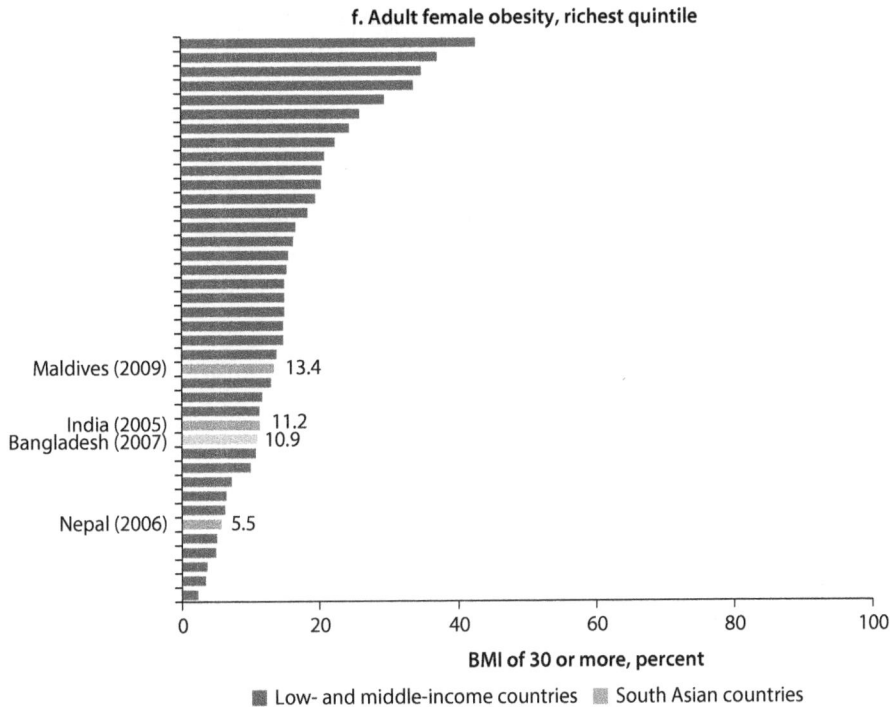

f. Adult female obesity, richest quintile

Maldives (2009) — 13.4
India (2005) — 11.2
Bangladesh (2007) — 10.9
Nepal (2006) — 5.5

BMI of 30 or more, percent

■ Low- and middle-income countries ■ South Asian countries

Source: Statistics from the World Health Organization Global Health Observatory Data Repository (accessed March 13, 2016), http://apps.who.int/gho/data/node.home.
Note: Figure includes low- and middle-income countries with statistics for the indicators in the period 2005–09.
BMI = body mass index.

Figure 1.7 Urban-Rural Differences in Selected Child Health and Nutrition Outcomes in Bangladesh, mid-1990s to 2014

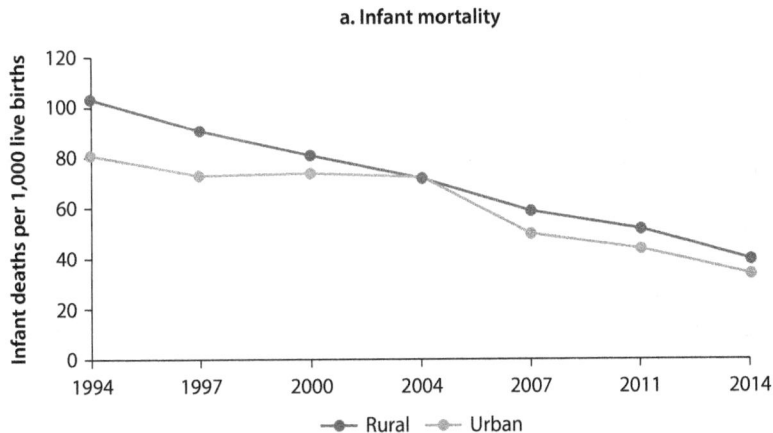

a. Infant mortality

Infant deaths per 1,000 live births

—●— Rural —●— Urban

figure continues next page

Figure 1.7 Urban-Rural Differences in Selected Child Health and Nutrition Outcomes in Bangladesh, mid-1990s to 2014 *(continued)*

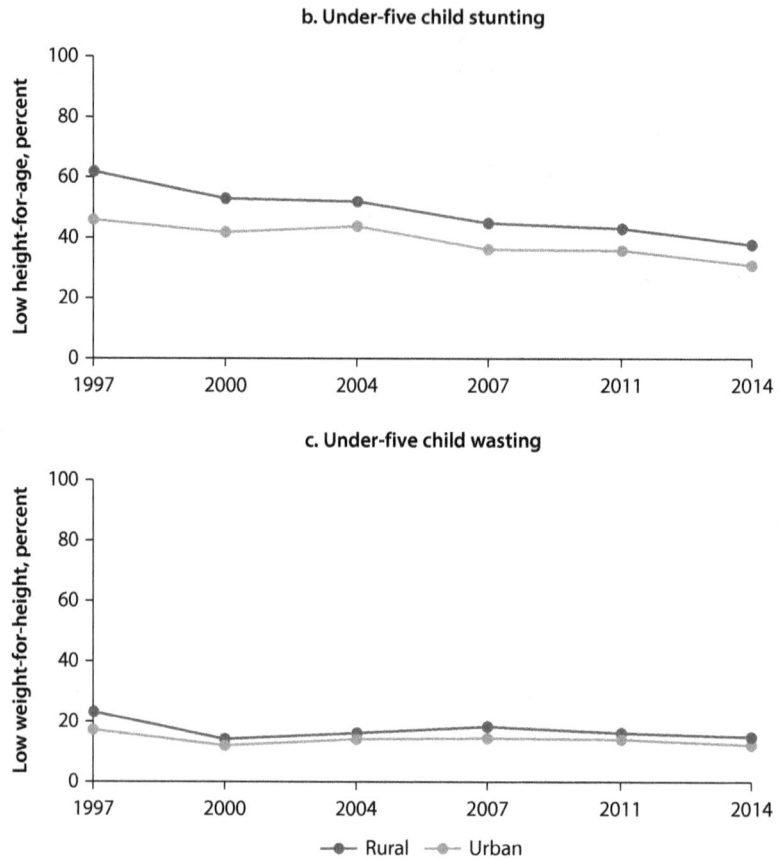

b. Under-five child stunting

c. Under-five child wasting

Sources: Infant mortality statistics from Bangladesh Demographic and Health Survey (DHS) reports for 1993–94, 1996–97, 1999–2000, 2004, 2007, 2011, and 2014. Under-five stunting and wasting rates are World Bank estimates using DHS data for 1993–94, 1996–97, 1999–2000, 2004, 2007, and 2011.
Note: Child stunting and wasting rates for all survey years are based on the World Health Organization 2006 child growth standards: http://www.who.int/childgrowth/en/.

For adults, urban-rural patterns in average health outcomes differ by indicator. The 2011 DHS statistics indicate that both women and men are more likely to be underweight in rural areas, whereas they are more likely to be overweight and suffer from hypertension and diabetes in urban areas (figure 1.8).[11]

Urban Health Services

Urban governments are responsible for public health services (for example, sanitation, water supply, drainage, food safety and quality, vector-borne disease control, and public safety) and preventive and curative care through public hospitals, clinics, and dispensaries. Urban governments are also responsible for licensing private health providers. As noted earlier, the Ministry of Local Government,

Figure 1.8 Urban-Rural Differences in Selected Adult Health and Nutrition Outcomes in Bangladesh, by Gender, 2011

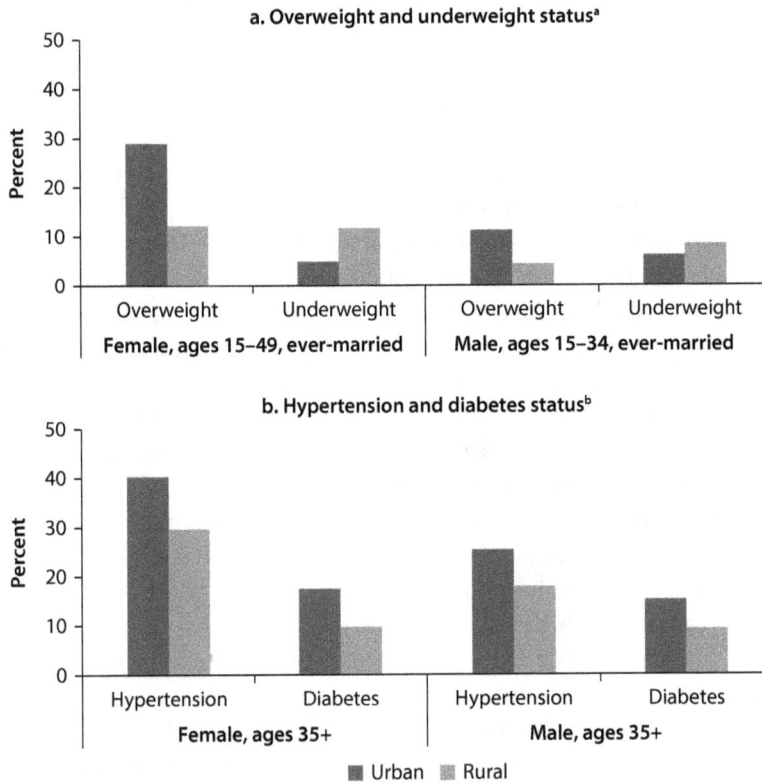

a. Overweight and underweight status[a]

b. Hypertension and diabetes status[b]

■ Urban ■ Rural

Source: Statistics from the 2011 Bangladesh Demographic and Health Survey report (NIPORT, Mitra and Associates, and ICF International 2013).
a. An individual is classified as "overweight" if the body mass index (BMI) is 25 or higher and "underweight" if the BMI is 17 or lower.
b. An individual is classified as having hypertension if he or she (a) has blood pressure equal to or exceeding 140 millimeters of mercury systolic blood pressure (SBP), (b) has blood pressure equal to or exceeding 90 millimeters of mercury diastolic blood pressure (DBP), or (c) is currently taking antihypertensive medication. An individual is classified as having diabetes if he or she reports taking medication for diabetes or has fasting blood glucose equal to or exceeding 7.0 millimoles per liter.

Rural Development and Co-operatives, through its Local Government Division, supports urban governments in these tasks by providing financial and human resources. MOHFW is responsible for national health and family planning standards, strategy and policy development, and regulation, as well as secondary and tertiary care through its own public hospitals in city corporations and municipal cities and towns (Adams, Islam, and Ahmed 2015; ICDDR,B 2015).

Institutional reviews posit several interrelated issues that are perceived to hamper Bangladesh's urban public health care services (Afsana and Wahid 2013; ICDRR,B 2015):

• Poor planning and management capacity
• Poor coordination between the various authorities

- Lack of clear, separate roles and responsibilities for the various authorities
- Major service coverage gaps
- Human resource management issues such as chronic and acute understaffing, low staff competency, and low staff effort

Overarching all of these challenges, public health services appear to be under-prioritized by urban governments. City corporations and municipal governments are legislated to perform 248 and 172 distinct tasks, respectively. In practice, they focus on a much more limited set of tasks such as waste disposal, street lighting, and road and drain maintenance (Rahman and Ahmed 2015).

Although nongovernmental organizations (NGOs) have traditionally played a major role in providing development services in rural Bangladesh, they have more recently expanded their presence and role in urban areas. Urban govern-ments have contracted out the operation of most public primary health facilities to NGOs, which also operate their own facilities. These NGO facilities, whether owned or contracted, tend to serve the poor, providing subsidized or free care (Adams, Islam, and Ahmed 2015). NGO and public health facilities are virtually the only providers of family planning (especially long-term methods) and mater-nal and child health services. Urban governments and NGOs also deploy com-munity health workers in poor neighborhoods for health promotion and preventive care outreach.[12]

Private providers, which are fee-based and for-profit, include hospitals, clinics, nursing homes, diagnostic centers, and pharmacies as well as private practices by medical doctors and nonformal or traditional health practitioners. Private pro-viders tend to provide curative care. They also tend to operate without required licenses and have health service staff lacking required academic and professional qualifications (ICDDR,B 2015).[13] Compared with health service staff in public and NGO facilities, private providers are less likely to know government guide-lines for health service practice management (ICDDR,B 2015).

However, private facilities are more accessible than public and NGO facilities because of their widespread service coverage and longer, more convenient service hours. Many private providers offer services at low fees, making them affordable to the poor, especially when the various monetary and nonmonetary costs of traveling to farther-off public and NGO facilities are factored in (Adams, Islam, and Ahmed 2015; Afsana and Wahid 2013).

As for health service demand by and supply to the poor, slum residents in Dhaka report that they prefer to seek health services from pharmacies and non-formal or traditional health service practitioners, and they prefer home deliveries by traditional birth attendants (Adams, Islam, and Ahmed 2015). These findings are consistent with other evidence for Bangladesh (as well as many other LMICs) that the poor tend to obtain care from informal private health service practitioners—that is, those who lack required academic and professional quali-fications or are unlicensed to practice (Sudhinaraset and others 2013).

A census of health service providers in or near a sample of slum settlements in Dhaka found that more than 80 percent were private providers, 12 percent were public facilities (but with operations contracted out to NGOs), and 6 percent were NGO facilities (Adams, Islam, and Ahmed 2015). Thirty-eight percent of the private providers were pharmacies, while 35 percent were non-formal or traditional health service practitioners. More than 60 percent of private health service staff were unqualified compared with 2 percent of public health service staff. Half of the NGO health service staff were community health workers.

Rigorous, representative evidence on provider quality of care and its determinants are absent for urban Bangladesh. Among the available evidence, sample users in Dhaka rated private hospitals higher than public hospitals in terms of responsiveness, communication, and discipline (Andaleeb 2000). In Sylhet, user satisfaction with NGO primary health facilities was driven by perceived provider professionalism, courtesy, and low-cost or free services (Gazi and others 2015). And a qualitative study of NGO delivery centers in Dhaka slum settlements found that (a) service performance varied markedly across centers, (b) the retention and effort of community health workers were key factors associated with center service performance, and (c) center hygiene and free services were key factors associated with center use (Banu and Nasreen 2011).[14]

To the best of our knowledge, rigorous evidence is nonexistent regarding health service staff absenteeism from facilities in urban Bangladesh as well as what health service staff are doing when present at facilities. As for rural Bangladesh, evidence from public primary health facilities indicates high rates of staff vacancies and staff absence, particularly among doctors (Chaudhury and Hammer 2004).

Likewise, to the best of our knowledge, direct measures of health service quality are absent for either urban or rural Bangladesh. Audit-study evidence from rural and urban India suggests that the quality of care—measured by, for example, completion of checklists for essential and recommended care, correct diagnosis, and correct treatment—was low in both public and private primary health clinics (Das and others 2012). At the same time, factors such as medical equipment, doctor qualifications, and patient caseloads were either not associated or only weakly associated with quality of care. Although private doctors in India tend to be unqualified, they exerted greater effort and performed no worse on diagnosis and treatment than qualified public doctors (Das and others 2012, 2016). Qualified public doctors exerted greater effort and were more likely to provide correct treatment in their private practices than in their public practices (Das and others 2016). These issues are suspected to also exist in urban Bangladesh.

Notes

1. For the current 2018 fiscal year, low-income economies are defined as those with a gross national income (GNI) per capita, calculated using the World Bank Atlas method, of US$1,005 or less in 2016; lower-middle-income economies are those with a GNI per capita of US$1,006–US$3,955; upper-middle-income economies are those with a GNI per capita of US$3,956–US$12,235; and high-income economies are

those with a GNI per capita of US$12,236 or more ("World Bank Country and Lending Groups," World Bank Open Data Portal, https://datahelpdesk.worldbank .org/knowledgebase/articles/906519-world-bank-country-and-lending-groups).

2. The agglomeration index is a measure of urban concentration based on three factors: population density, the size of the population in a "large" urban center, and travel time to that urban center (Uchida and Nelson 2009).

3. In the 1981, 1991, and 2001 censuses, the definition of an urban area included urban developments next to large cities. The 2011 redefinition, which excluded those adjacent developments, reduced the total area classified as urban from 10,711 square kilometers in 2001 to 8,867 square kilometers in 2011 (a 17 percent reduction). The reductions affected some districts more than others. In particular, Dhaka, Chittagong, Gazipur, and Khulna Districts experienced reductions in their urban areas of more than 50 percent (GOB 2014).

4. The 2010–11 Bangladesh Household Income and Expenditure Survey (HIES) drew data from the 2001 census as the sampling frame and used the pre-2011 definition of an urban area. An estimated 27 percent of the country's population was urban based on these data.

5. Mymensingh Division, the eighth division, was formed in 2015, divided from Dhaka Division.

6. While poverty incidence refers to the basic poverty headcount (percentage of the population that is poor), the depth of poverty (also called the "poverty gap") is the average percentage by which individuals fall below the poverty line. The poverty severity index (also called "poverty intensity") is calculated as the poverty gap index squared; it implicitly gives greater weight to the poorest individuals, making it a combined measure of poverty and income inequality. These three poverty metrics are known as the Foster–Greer–Thorbecke (FGT) indexes (Foster, Greer, and Thorbecke 1984).

7. The Gini coefficient is the most common measure of the inequality of income (or consumption) distribution within a country. A Gini value of 0 indicates full equality, and 1 indicates maximum inequality.

8. A settlement was defined to be slum if it had at least 10 households and met four of the following five conditions: poor housing quality, high population density or overcrowded housing, poor water supply and sanitation facilities, insecure tenure, and a majority of households that are poor.

9. Although the statistics from the 2005 and 2014 censuses are not directly comparable, the basic message is the same: slum settlements and their populations are a major feature of urban Bangladesh.

10. Although analogous figures for rural Bangladesh are not produced, the noted international rank patterns for urban Bangladesh also apply to rural Bangladesh, suggesting that the patterns apply to Bangladesh as a whole.

11. Although published statistics from the 2014 DHS are available, statistics from the 2011 DHS are reported in figure 1.8 because health and nutrition data were collected for a wider adult sample in 2011. The 2014 DHS measured only height and weight for women, and measured blood pressure and took blood samples for a selected sample of women with a live birth in the preceding three years.

12. Community health workers in villages are credited for the notable declines in fertility and maternal and child mortality as well as gains in child vaccination rates and uptake of oral rehydration therapy in Bangladesh (El Arifeen and others 2013).

13. Private health care staff report that they often obtain their health knowledge either through NGO training courses or by learning on the job under the guidance of other staff (Adams, Islam, and Ahmed 2015).

14. Among a sample of NGO female volunteer community health workers in Dhaka, intermediate indicators of worker retention and job effort were associated with financial rewards and, to a lesser degree, with social recognition and positive community feedback (Alam, Tasneem, and Oliveras 2012a, 2012b).

References

Adams, Alayne M., Rubana Islam, and Tanvir Ahmed. 2015. "Who Serves the Urban Poor? A Geospatial and Descriptive Analysis of Health Services in Slum Settlements in Dhaka, Bangladesh." *Health Policy and Planning* 30 (Suppl 1): i32– i45.

Afsana, Kaosar, and Syed Shabab Wahid. 2013. "Health Care for Poor People in the Urban Slums of Bangladesh." *Lancet* 382 (9910): 2049–51.

Alam, Khurshid, Sakiba Tasneem, and Elizabeth Oliveras. 2012a. "Performance of Female Volunteer Community Health Workers in Dhaka Urban Slums." *Social Science and Medicine* 75 (3): 511–15.

———. 2012b. "Retention of Female Volunteer Community Health Workers in Dhaka Urban Slums: A Case Control Study." *Health Policy and Planning* 27 (6): 477–86.

Andaleeb, Syed Saad. 2000. "Public and Private Hospitals in Bangladesh: Service Quality and Predictors of Hospital Choice." *Health Policy and Planning* 15 (1): 95–102.

Angeles, Gustavo, Peter Lance, Janine Barden-O'Fallon, Nazrul Islam, A. Q. M. Mahbub, and Nurul Islam Nazem. 2009. "The 2005 Census and Mapping of Slums in Bangladesh: Design, Select Results and Application." *International Journal of Health Geographics* 8 (32).

Banu, Morsheda, and Hashima E. Nasreen. 2011. "Factors Influencing the Performance of Delivery Centers in Urban Slums of Bangladesh: A Qualitative Study." *OIDA International Journal of Sustainable Development* 2 (12): 67–76.

Chaudhury, Nazmul, and Jeffrey S. Hammer. 2004. "Ghost Doctors: Absenteeism in Rural Bangladeshi Health Facilities." *World Bank Economic Review* 18 (3): 423–41.

Das, Jishnu, Alaka Holla, Veena Das, Manoj Mohanan, Diana Tabak, and Brian Chan. 2012. "In Urban and Rural India, a Standardized Patient Study Showed Low Levels of Provider Training and Huge Quality Gaps." *Health Affairs* 32 (12): 2774–84.

Das, Jishnu, Alaka Holla, Aakash Mohpal, and Karthik Muralidharan. 2016. "Quality and Accountability in Health Care Delivery: Audit-Study Evidence from Primary Care in India." *American Economic Review* 106 (12): 3765–99.

El Arifeen, Shams, Aliki Christou, Laura Reichenbach, Ferdous Arfina Osman, Kishwar Azad, Khaled Shamsul Islam, Faruque Ahmed, Henry B. Perry, and David H. Peters. 2013. "Community-Based Approaches and Partnerships: Innovations in Health-Service Delivery in Bangladesh." *Lancet* 382 (9909): 2012–26.

Ellis, Peter, and Mark Roberts. 2016. *Leveraging Urbanization in South Asia: Managing Spatial Transformation for Prosperity and Livability.* South Asia Development Matters Series. Washington, DC: World Bank.

Foster, James, Joel Greer, and Erik Thorbecke. 1984. "A Class of Decomposable Poverty Measures." *Econometrica* 3 (52): 761–66.

Gazi, Rukhsana, Marufa Sultana, Humayun Kabir, and Nirod Chandra Saha. 2015. "Accessibility, Availability and Perceived Quality of Reproductive Health Services in Selected Urban Areas of Bangladesh: User and Non Users' Perspectives." *Reproductive System & Sexual Disorders* 4 (3): 154.

GOB (Government of Bangladesh). 2011. *Report of the Household Income & Expenditure Survey 2010*. Dhaka: Bangladesh Bureau of Statistics, GOB.

———. 2014. *Bangladesh Population & Housing Census 2011—National Volume-3: Urban Area Report*. Dhaka: Bangladesh Bureau of Statistics, GOB.

———. 2015. "Preliminary Report on the Census of Slum Areas and Floating Population 2014." Report, Bangladesh Bureau of Statistics, GOB, Dhaka.

Hossain, M. A., M. Moniruzzaman, and M. A. Islam. 2010. "Urban Environmental Health in Bangladesh Slum: A Comparative Study of Two Metropolitan Cities." *Journal of Science Foundation* 8 (1–2): 67–76.

ICDDR,B (International Center for Diarrheal Disease Research, Bangladesh). 2015. "Technical Assistance for Assessment of Contribution of Ministry of Health and Family Welfare for Urban Health Services." ICDDR,B, Dhaka.

Islam, Md. Rezaul, Md. Farukuzzaman, and Md. Amirul Islam. 2014. "Situation of Slum's Children in Dhaka City, Bangladesh: A Sample Survey." *Journal of Economics and Sustainable Development* 5 (18): 27–33.

Kaufmann, Daniel, Aart Kraay, and Massimo Mastruzzi. 2007. "The Worldwide Governance Indicators Project: Answering the Critics." Policy Research Working Paper No. 4149, World Bank, Washington, DC. https://openknowledge.worldbank.org/handle/10986/7203.

Marx, Benjamin, Thomas Stoker, and Tavneet Suri. 2013. "The Economics of Slums in the Developing World." *Journal of Economic Perspectives* 27 (4): 187–210.

Nahar, Samsun, and M. Maksudur Rahman. 2013. "Factors Influencing Health and Healthcare Delivery System for the Urban Poor in Chittagong City, Bangladesh." *Asian Journal of Management Research* 4 (2): 288–96.

NIPORT (National Institute of Population Research and Training), Mitra and Associates, and ICF International. 2013. "Bangladesh Demographic and Health Survey 2011." Dhaka, Bangladesh; Calverton, MD: NIPORT, Mitra and Associates, and ICF International.

Rahman, Hossain Zillur, and Tofail Ahmed. 2015. "Strategy on Local Government Strengthening: Background Paper for 7th Five Year Plan." Background paper, Power and Participation Research Center, Dhaka.

Sudhinaraset, May, Matthew Ingram, Heather K. Lofthouse, and Dominic Montagu. 2013. "What Is the Role of Informal Healthcare Providers in Developing Countries? A Systematic Review." *PLoS One* 8 (2): e54978.

Uchida, Hirotsugu, and Andrew Nelson. 2009. "Agglomeration Index: Towards a New Measure of Urban Concentration." Background paper for *World Development Report 2009: Reshaping Economic Geography*. Washington, DC: World Bank.

UN DESA (United Nations Department of Economic and Social Affairs). 2015. *World Urbanization Prospects: The 2014 Revision*. New York: United Nations.

UN-Habitat (United Nations Human Settlements Programme). 2016. *World Cities Report 2016. Urbanization and Development: Emerging Futures*. Nairobi, Kenya: UN-Habitat.

Van de Poel, E., O. O'Donnell, and E. Van Doorslaer. 2007. "Are Urban Children Really Healthier? Evidence from 47 Developing Countries." *Social Science & Medicine* 65 (10): 1986–2003.

WHO (World Health Organization). 2010. *A Conceptual Framework for Action on the Social Determinants of Health* (Social Determinants of Health Discussion Paper 2). Geneva: WHO.

World Bank. 2013. "Bangladesh Poverty Assessment: Assessing a Decade of Progress in Reducing Poverty 2000–2010." Bangladesh Development Series Paper No. 31, World Bank, Dhaka.

———. 2016. *World Development Indicators 2016*. Washington, DC: World Bank.

CHAPTER 2

Analytical Approach

Quantitative Analysis of Social Determinants of Health and Nutrition in Bangladesh's Cities

The study's quantitative analysis examines the variation in adult and child health and nutrition in Bangladesh's city corporations. It includes a basic analysis of a wide set of adult and child health and nutrition outcomes as well as a deeper analysis of adult underweight, overweight, and mental health statuses and the nutrition status of children under age five, measured by child height-for-age. The main question concerns which individual, household, and neighborhood-area factors are associated with child and adult health and nutrition status. The question is examined for all residents in city corporations as well as separately for slum and nonslum residents.

Past empirical research in low- and middle-income countries (LMICs) has been limited by the lack of representative data between and within urban areas. In the case of Bangladesh, health studies have used national household survey samples to examine either (a) urban-rural differences in health and nutrition, or (b) overall urban health and nutrition (treating urban areas as an undifferentiated whole) (see, for example, Srinivasan, Zanello, and Shankar 2013). Other studies have used small-scale convenience or purposive samples of individuals, households, or facilities to examine health and nutrition in specific cities and towns (for example, Dhaka and Chittagong) or in specific subpopulations within cities and towns (for example, slum residents) (see, for example, Choudhury and others 2012).

The data situation is changing, and Bangladesh is a relative forerunner. In 2006, the National Institute of Population Research and Training (NIPORT) and others conducted the Bangladesh Urban Health Survey (BUHS), providing, for the first time, extensive data on adult and child health and nutrition outcomes and potentially relevant factors that are representative for slum and nonslum areas in city corporations as well as for district municipalities and large towns (NIPORT and others 2008). In 2013, the survey was repeated on a new cross-section that is representative for the same domains (NIPORT and others 2015). The two rounds of the BUHS serve as the data sources for the study.

Rationale for Focus on Slum Residents

The study investigates patterns and determinants of urban health and nutrition outcomes, with a focus on differences between slum and nonslum residents. The health and nutrition status of slum residents are of interest for several reasons:

- *Theory and empirical evidence suggest that the study of slum health and nutrition should be treated as distinct from the study of urban health or the study of poverty and health (Ezeh and others 2017).* One argument for the separate treatment is that the physical and social environments of slums may amplify the residents' health risks and produce negative health externalities that extend across a slum settlement or even more widely. The exposure to concentrated health risks in slum settlements may be particularly harmful to young children, given that they are more immunologically susceptible than older children and adults. Marx, Stoker, and Suri (2013) argue that the potential adverse health effects of slum settlements may create a low human-capital equilibrium that, in turn, contributes to making slum settlements into poverty traps.
- *The scant available literature on slum health and nutrition points to patterns that require deeper investigation.*[1] For example, the evidence indicates that the average health and nutrition outcomes of slum residents are worse than those of nonslum residents, and are often worse than those of rural residents, indicating that the so-called urban health advantage does not appear to apply to slum residents (Ezeh and others 2017; Mberu and others 2016).
- *Research on the health risks and effects of slum settlements has policy implications.* Such research is needed to guide the design and implementation of policies and interventions related to slum development in general and slum health in particular (Lilford and others 2017).

Selection of Child Health and Nutrition Outcomes

Child height-for-age is widely regarded as the most relevant measure of overall child nutrition status, and child stunting (a height-for-age z-score [HAZ] that is more than two standard deviations below the international reference median, based on 2006 World Health Organization [WHO] child growth standards)[2] is considered the key indicator for tracking progress in addressing child undernutrition. The child stunting rate is one of two child nutrition indicators selected to measure progress against UN (United Nations) Sustainable Development Goal 2, Target 2.2: "By 2030, end all forms of malnutrition, including achieving, by 2025, the internationally agreed targets on stunting and wasting in children under 5 years of age" (UN 2015).

Child stunting reflects the cumulative effects of poor diet and recurrent infection. Globally in 2004, 15 percent of deaths and another 15 percent of the burden of disease for children under five years of age were attributed to stunting (Black and others 2008). International evidence indicates that child stunting is associated with (a) lower motor, cognitive, emotional, and social development; (b) higher rates of illness, disability, and premature death; and (c) poorer socioeconomic outcomes in adolescence and adulthood, measured by, for example, education attainment, student academic achievement, employment, and labor earnings (Black and others 2013; Currie and Vogl 2013; Victora and others 2008).

Selection of Adult Health and Nutrition Outcomes

The motivation for the in-depth analysis of adult overweight status, underweight status, and mental ill-health scores is threefold: First, the outcomes are already determined to be, or are emerging as, important risks behind mortality and morbidity in LMICs (Black and others 2008; Murray and others 2012; Whiteford and others 2013). Second, the averages for these outcomes differ between slum and nonslum residents. Third, the outcomes are relatively understudied in LMICs, but they are garnering greater attention from national health policy makers, practitioners, and international donors. As a case in point, the health-related UN Sustainable Development Goals explicitly refer to noncommunicable diseases and mental health (UN 2015).

Data and Sample

The 2006 and 2013 BUHS rounds were designed to provide data that were representative of three urban areas: slum neighborhoods in city corporations, nonslum neighborhoods in city corporations, and municipal cities and towns. The 2006 BUHS covered the 6 city corporations existing at that time, and the 2013 BUHS covered 10 of the 11 city corporations existing in 2013.[3]

The sample frame for the survey was a complete list of mahallas in the city corporations and sampled municipal cities and towns. (A mahalla is an Islamic parish and an optional, nonelective administrative unit below the ward in Bangladesh cities and towns.) In city corporations, neighborhoods were randomly selected in the first stage of sampling. In each sampled neighborhood, all slum and nonslum areas were mapped through visits. An area was defined as a "slum settlement" if it had at least 10 households and met four of five conditions: poor housing conditions, insecure housing tenure, high population density, poor sanitation and inadequate water access, and over 75 percent of households appearing to be poor. The second stage of sampling differed slightly between the 2006 and 2013 rounds, but slum and nonslum areas of sampled neighborhoods (the primary sampling units) were randomly drawn, stratified by slum status. The primary sampling unit is referred to as "neighborhood area."

Given the interest in understanding slum-nonslum differences in average health and nutrition status, district municipalities and large towns were excluded from the analysis. Based on the 2011 census, the city corporations in the 2006 and 2013 survey rounds accounted for 38 percent and 41 percent of the country's urban population, respectively. The 2006 survey round collected data on several adult and child health and nutrition outcomes. The 2013 survey round collected data on fewer child health and nutrition outcomes (specifically, child anthropometry, recent fever, and recent acute respiratory infection [ARI] symptoms) but did not collect any data on adult health and nutrition outcomes. Given this, the study examines adult health and nutrition outcomes using the 2006 survey round and child HAZ using the 2013 survey round. Child fever and ARI symptoms are examined as potential determinants of child HAZ.

Unless otherwise specified, the child sample for analysis is restricted to children aged 0–59 months. Health and anthropometry data were collected for this age group only. The adult samples for analysis are restricted to women and men aged 18–49 years who had ever been married. The ever-married restriction and the age ceiling of 49 years are data driven. Some factors, such as own or joint authority over household decisions, were collected only for adults up to age 49 years. In line with the legal age of adulthood in Bangladesh, the age floor for the adult analysis is set at 18 years. The shares of women and men aged 18–49 years who have ever been married are 88 percent and 68 percent, respectively.

The actual age range for the adult analysis depends on the health outcome data. For example, data for constructing rates of overweight, underweight, hypertensive, and diabetic adults were collected only for women and men aged 35–59 years. For these outcomes, the adult analysis is restricted to ever-married women and men aged 35–49 years.

The mental health measure for women and men is specially constructed. The female and male BUHS questionnaires in 2006 asked a battery of 20 questions related to mental problems experienced in the preceding 30 days. The questions are from the Self-Reporting Questionnaire (SRQ20) developed by WHO to screen for depression- and anxiety-related symptoms, particularly in low-income settings (WHO 1994). Responses to the questions are either yes or no. The number of yeses were totaled to arrive at a mental ill-health score from 0 to 20. There is no internationally recommended score cutoff that indicates probable mental disorder. WHO advises that the score cutoff for a setting be determined after validating the SRQ20 instrument in that setting, which was not performed for the BUHS setting. Thus, the mental ill-health scores as a continuous variable were used for the analysis, logging values to reduce the degree of right skewness in the outcome distribution (zeros were set to 0.1 before the log transformation).

Empirical Strategy

The study first estimates average levels for virtually all health and nutrition outcomes in the BUHS data. It then estimates average levels for an extensive set of demographic and socioeconomic factors that serve as potential determinants in health and nutrition regressions. The study estimates average outcomes and factors for all city corporation residents as well as separately for slum and nonslum residents in city corporations.

The study then estimates regressions to examine the conditional average relationship between health and nutrition outcomes and factors in the full, slum, and nonslum samples. For continuous outcomes, the regression relationships are modeled as linear, based on ordinary least squares. For dichotomous outcomes, the regression relationships are modeled as nonlinear, following a logistic cumulative distribution function and estimated via maximum likelihood. Estimated logit model parameters (and standard errors) are transformed into odds ratios.

To avoid a problem with inference due to potential multicolinearity in the regression analysis for adult health and nutrition outcomes, some factors were combined into index variables based on principal component analysis. For each set of factors combined this way, the derived first component was used, which accounts for most of the variation across the included set of factors. Index variables were constructed for individual decision-making authority, housing quality, and neighborhood environmental quality, as follows:

- *Decision-making authority index:* For this individual-level variable, data were combined concerning whether the individual has own or joint decision-making authority over own health services, children's health services, large household purchases, purchases for daily needs, visits to relatives and friends, and food to cook. Separate decision-making authority index variables were constructed for women and men.
- *Housing quality index:* For this household-level variable, data were combined regarding flooring, roofing, walls, drinking water source, improved toilet facility, safe garbage disposal, and clean fuel for cooking.
- *Neighborhood quality index:* Data were combined on the presence of polluting manufacturing units, residential tenure security, sewerage, flooding, water supply, garbage collection, public electrical safety, and public safety in the neighborhood.

The derived first principal component for the decision-making authority index construction accounts for 44–62 percent of the variation across the included covariates, depending on the sample. For the housing quality index, the first principal component accounts for 43 percent of the variation. For the neighborhood quality index, the first principal component accounts for 19 percent of the variation. All index variables are standardized, with zero average and unit variance. A higher value in the relevant index implies own or joint authority over a wider set of household decisions, better housing quality, or better neighborhood environmental quality.

Qualitative Analysis of Urban Health Sector Governance

Definitions

For the qualitative analysis of urban health governance, governance is defined as "the rules that distribute roles and responsibilities among societal actors and that shape interactions among them" (Brinkerhoff and Bossert 2008). These rules can be both formal (embodied in institutions) and informal (reflected in behavioral patterns). Governance in health systems is therefore about developing and putting in place effective rules and norms for policies and programs aimed at achieving health sector objectives. While maintaining simplicity, this definition allows us the flexibility to look at what is a key determinant of poor performance of the health system in urban areas: de jure and de facto relationships among the relevant actors.

Strategy

The qualitative analysis explores specifically the urban health sector governance architecture in Bangladesh, and constraints to good governance, by analyzing the relationships among three sets of actors relevant to urban health service delivery—the government, service providers, and citizens—based on the *World Development Report 2004* framework (World Bank 2003), as shown in figure 2.1.

Among *state-level actors*, the focus is primarily on central and local government entities that have a direct responsibility for the organization, regulation, quality control, monitoring, and provision of health services to the urban population. With respect to *service providers*, the study examines the roles that different types of providers play in service delivery for the urban poor. Finally, with respect to *citizens*, the study considers the mechanisms by which citizens can hold both the government and the service providers accountable as well as the mechanisms they are using to make (informed) choices about where to seek care.

The study illustrates the current institutional arrangements, de jure and de facto roles and relationships, and division of responsibilities between the three groups of actors. It also explores how these roles, relationships, and responsibilities could influence different dimensions of urban health system performance, such as effectiveness, quality, equity, and affordability. The intent is to better understand successful experiences, as well as areas for improvement,

Figure 2.1 Health Governance Conceptual Framework

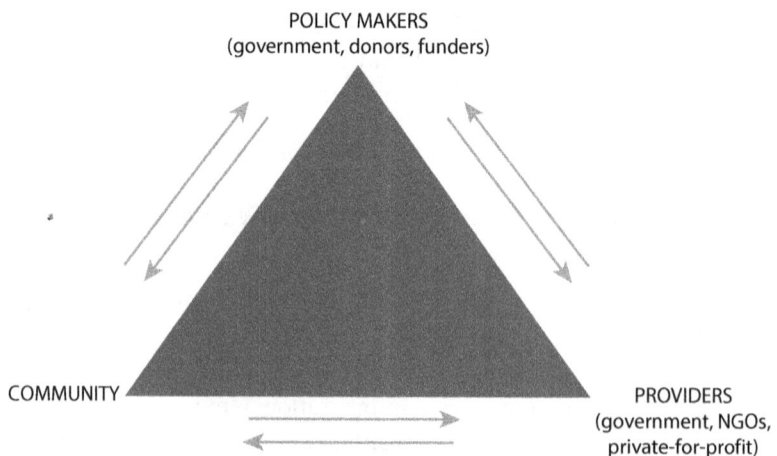

POLICY MAKERS
(government, donors, funders)

COMMUNITY

PROVIDERS
(government, NGOs,
private-for-profit)

Source: ©World Bank. Permission required for reuse.
Note: NGOs = nongovernmental organizations.

and formulate policy options that can help improve the urban health system and, ultimately, the health and nutrition outcomes of urban residents, particularly among the poor.

Data

The qualitative analysis draws on both primary and secondary information. It reviews existing regulations, policy documents, research studies, and available secondary qualitative and quantitative information. The primary information was collected between February 2016 and February 2017 through a combination of semistructured interviews (105) and focus groups discussions (25) with key informants and representatives of government officials, service providers, and citizens. The sampling of interviewees and focus group participants aimed to reach, to the extent feasible, all relevant individuals who could provide insights into the research questions. In addition, snowball sampling techniques were used to identify further interviewees and focus group participants based on referrals from those who had already participated in the study.

To ensure variety in our sampling and to capture different facets of urban health governance, data were collected in a sample of small, medium-size, and large cities in Bangladesh, selected based on accessibility to informants. Interview and focus group guides were developed to serve as starting points for the primary data collection. These tools were informed by the health governance conceptual framework and the information from secondary data, as well as the research team's background knowledge on the topic. The tools were piloted in the early stages of data collection and were adjusted to target each of three groups of actors. Multiple interviewers conducted the first stage of data collection to ensure consistency in future data collection rounds. Interview and focus group transcripts were maintained, but the references were anonymized.

Analysis

The data analysis was done systematically, using a combination of deductive and inductive approaches. The research team met repeatedly during data collection to identify themes emerging from the data (thematic analysis), which also helped guide future rounds of information collection. In accordance with the chosen analytical framework, the analysis looks at the roles of government, service providers, and citizens in the urban health system and identifies key constraints to effective governance.

To further validate the analysis, the report team shared the research plan, as well as the findings, at various points with the team's advisory panel and with selected informants before finalizing the qualitative study, documenting all steps of the research.

Based on the conceptual and methodological approaches just described, the next chapters will present the findings from the quantitative analysis of the social determinants of health and nutrition (chapter 3) and from the qualitative analysis of urban health governance (chapter 4).

Notes

1. For a recent review, see, for example, Ezeh and others (2017).
2. For more information about the WHO child growth standards, see http://www.who
.int/childgrowth/en/.
3. The 2006 BUHS included Barisal, Chittagong, Dhaka, Khulna, Rajshahi, and Sylhet
in the city corporation statistical domain. The 2013 BUHS included Barisal,
Chittagong, Comilla, Dhaka North, Dhaka South, Khulna, Narayanganj, Rajshahi,
Rangpur, and Sylhet in the city corporation statistical domain.

References

Black, Robert E., Lindsay H. Allen, Zulfiqar A. Bhutta, Laura. E. Caulfield, Mercedes de
Onis, Majid Ezzati, Colin Mathers, and Juan Rivera. 2008. "Maternal and Child
Undernutrition: Global and Regional Exposures and Health Consequences." *Lancet*
371 (9608): 243–60.

Black, Robert E., Cesar G. Victora, Susan P. Walker, Zulfiqar A. Bhutta, Parul Christian,
Mercedes de Onis, Majid Ezzati, Sally Grantham-McGregor, Joanne Katz, Reynaldo
Martorell, Ricardo Uauy, and the Maternal and Child Nutrition Study Group. 2013.
"Maternal and Child Undernutrition and Overweight in Low-Income and Middle-
Income Countries." *Lancet* 382 (9890): 427–51.

Brinkerhoff, Derick W., and Thomas J. Bossert. 2008. "Health Governance: Concepts,
Experience, and Programming Options." Policy Brief, Health Systems 20/20 Project,
U.S. Agency for International Development, Washington, DC.

Choudhury, Nuzhat, Allisyn C. Moran, M. Ashraful Alam, Karar Zunaid Ahsan,
Sabina F. Rashid, and Peter Kim Streatfield. 2012. "Beliefs and Practices during
Pregnancy and Childbirth in Urban Slums of Dhaka, Bangladesh." *BMC Public
Health* 12 (1): 791.

Currie, Janet, and Tom Vogl. 2013. "Early-Life Health and Adult Circumstance in
Developing Countries." *Annual Review of Economics* 5 (1): 1–36.

Ezeh, Alex, Oyinlola Oyebode, David Satterthwaite, Yen-Fu Chen, Robert Ndugwa, Jo
Sartori, Blessing Mberu, G. J. Melendez-Torres, Tilahun Haregu, Samuel I. Watson,
Waleska Caiaffa, Anthony Capon, and Richard J. Lilford. 2017. "The History,
Geography, and Sociology of Slums and the Health Problems of People Who Live in
Slums." *Lancet* 389 (10068): 547–58.

Lilford, Richard J., Oyinlola Oyebode, David Satterthwaite, G. J. Melendez-Torres,
Yen-Fu Chen, Blessing Mberu, Samuel I. Watson, Jo Sartori, Robert Ndugwa, Waleska
Caiaffa, Tilahun Haregu, Anthony Capon, Ruhi Saith, and Alex Ezeh. 2017.
"Improving the Health and Welfare of People Who Live in Slums." *Lancet* 389
(10068): 559–70.

Marx, Benjamin, Thomas Stoker, and Tavneet Suri. 2013. "The Economics of Slums in the
Developing World." *Journal of Economic Perspectives* 27 (4): 187–210.

Mberu, Blessing U., Tilahun N. Haregu, Catherine Kyobutungi, and Alex C. Ezeh. 2016.
"Health and Health-Related Indicators in Slum, Rural, and Urban Communities:
A Comparative Analysis." *Global Health Action* 9: 33163.

Murray, C. J., and others. 2012. "Disability-Adjusted Life Years (DALYs) for 291 Diseases
and Injuries in 21 Regions, 1990–2010: A Systematic Analysis for the Global Burden
of Disease Study 2010." *Lancet* 380 (9859): 2197–223.

NIPORT (National Institute of Population Research and Training), MEASURE Evaluation, ICDDR,B (International Center for Diarrheal Disease Research, Bangladesh), and ACPR (Associates for Community and Population Research). 2008. *2006 Bangladesh Urban Health Survey*. Dhaka, Bangladesh; Chapel Hill, NC: NIPORT, MEASURE Evaluation, ICDDRB, and ACPR.

———. 2015. "Bangladesh Urban Health Survey 2013." Final Report, MEASURE Evaluation, Chapel Hill, NC.

Rahman, Hossain Zillur, and Tofail Ahmed. 2015. "Strategy on Local Government Strengthening: Background Paper for 7th Five Year Plan." Background paper, Power and Participation Research Center, Dhaka.

Srinivasan, Chittur S., Giacomo Zanello, and Bhavani Shankar. 2013. "Rural-Urban Disparities in Child Nutrition in Bangladesh and Nepal." *BMC Public Health* 13: 581.

UN (United Nations). 2015. "Transforming Our World: The 2030 Agenda for Sustainable Development." A/RES/70/1, UN, New York.

Victora, Cesar G., Linda Adair, Caroline Fall, Pedro C. Hallal, Reynaldo Martorell, Linda Richter, and Harshpal Singh Sachdev. 2008. "Maternal and Child Undernutrition: Consequences for Adult Health and Human Capital." *Lancet* 371 (9609): 340–57.

Whiteford, H. A., L. Degenhardt, J. Rehm, A. J. Baxter, A. J. Ferrari, H. E. Erskine, F. J. Charlson, R. E. Norman, A. D. Flaxman, N. Johns, R. Burstein, C. J. Murray, and T. Vos. 2013. "Global Burden of Disease Attributable to Mental and Substance Use Disorders: Findings from the Global Burden of Disease Study 2010." *Lancet* 382 (9904): 1576–86.

WHO (World Health Organization). 1994. "A User's Guide to the Self Reporting Questionnaire (SRQ)." Document WHO/MNH/PSF/94.8, Division of Mental Health, WHO, Geneva.

World Bank. 2003. *World Development Report 2004: Making Services Work for Poor People.* Washington, DC: World Bank.

CHAPTER 3

Findings on the Social Determinants of Health and Nutrition Status in Bangladesh's Cities

Child Health and Nutrition Outcomes

We begin by reporting findings from examining child growth measured by child height-for-age z-scores (HAZ) for under-five children in city corporations, based on the 2013 Bangladesh Urban Health Study (BUHS) (NIPORT and others 2015).

Average Child Growth and Factor Levels

In the full sample of under-five children in city corporations, average HAZ was –1.69 standard deviations (SD) below the international reference median, the moderate-to-severe stunting rate was 42 percent, and the severe stunting rate was 20 percent (table 3.1).[1] Slum children in city corporations are significantly shorter than nonslum children: their average HAZ is 0.6 SD lower than that of nonslum children, their moderate-to-severe stunting rate is 16 percentage points lower, and their severe stunting rate is 10 percentage points lower.[2]

Comparing statistics for city corporations to published statistics from the 2014 Demographic and Health Survey (DHS) for rural and urban areas nationwide, three main findings are noted:

- City corporations have poorer average child growth outcomes than all urban areas. For example, the moderate-to-severe stunting rate in the full city corporation sample is 42 percent, compared with 31 percent in all urban areas.
- Slum children have poorer average growth outcomes than rural children. For example, the moderate-to-severe stunting rate for slum children is 48 percent, compared with 38 percent for rural children.
- Nonslum children have a lower moderate-to-severe stunting rate than rural children (31 percent versus 38 percent) but have a comparable severe stunting rate (13 percent versus 12 percent).

Table 3.1 Average Under-Five Child HAZ and Stunting Rates in Bangladesh, by Location Type

Indicator	City corporations (2013 BUHS)				National (2014 DHS)	
	Full (1)	Slum (2)	Nonslum (3)	Slum-nonslum (4)	Rural (5)	Urban (6)
Average HAZ	−1.69	−1.88	−1.30	−0.58***	−1.60	−1.30
Moderate-to-severe stunting (%)[a]	42	48	31	16***	38	31
Severe stunting (%)[b]	20	23	13	10***	12	10

Sources: Estimates based on data from the 2013 Bangladesh Urban Health Survey and the 2014 Bangladesh Demographic and Health Survey.
Note: Estimates are adjusted for sampling weights. Inference is based on robust standard errors, clustered at the neighborhood level.
BUHS = Bangladesh Urban Health Survey; DHS = Demographic and Health Survey; HAZ = height-for-age z-score.
a. "Moderate-to-severe stunting" = HAZ more than two standard deviations below the international reference population median.
b. "Severe stunting" = HAZ more than three standard deviations below the international reference population median.
*$p < 0.10$; **$p < 0.05$; ***$p < 0.01$.

The statistics suggest that average child growth outcomes in urban areas conceal substantial variation in average outcomes between and within urban centers, and that average outcomes are especially poor for slum children, not just as an urban subpopulation but also as a national subpopulation.

Average levels of child, mother, household, and neighborhood-area factors included in the multivariate analysis of child HAZ are as follows (table 3.2):[3]

- *Child factors:* In the full sample, 3 percent experienced an illness with acute respiratory infection (ARI) symptoms, and 31 percent experienced an illness with fever in the two weeks before the survey.
- *Mother factors:* Eighty-six percent of all children in the sample were born when their mothers were aged 18–34 years, an age range considered to have a lower risk of child death (Rustein and Winter 2014). Their mothers' average education attainment was 5.68 years, 20 percent had mothers who were currently employed, and 85 percent had mothers who were regularly exposed to mass media as measured by watching television at least once a week (television being the most popular mass media source).
- *Household factors:* Children lived in households with an average size of 4.87 members, and an average standardized wealth index of −0.36 SD.
- *Neighborhood-area factors:* Sixty-nine percent of children lived in areas with formal garbage collection, 48 percent in areas with a proper sewerage system, 51 percent in areas served by community health workers (CHWs), 48 percent in areas with an available nongovernmental organization (NGO) health facility, 14 percent in areas with an available public health facility, and 36 percent in areas with an available private health facility. All neighborhood areas had pharmacies.

Several factors were less favorable for slum children than for nonslum children: child health (recent illness with fever or ARI symptoms), mother's age at child's birth, mother's education attainment, mother's regular exposure to mass media, and formal garbage collection and proper sewerage system in the neighborhood area. In addition, the average household wealth index score was a standard deviation

Table 3.2 Average Levels of Factors in Under-Five Child HAZ in City Corporations, by Neighborhood-Area Type, 2013

Factor	Full (1)	Slum (2)	Nonslum (3)	Slum-nonslum (4)
a. Child				
Age (months)	30.12	30.08	30.20	–0.12
Female	0.49	0.49	0.50	–0.00
Birth order	2.06	2.16	1.87	0.29***
Ill with ARI symptoms	0.03	0.03	0.03	0.00
Ill with fever	0.31	0.33	0.28	0.05***
b. Mother				
Age at child's birth <18 years	0.09	0.11	0.07	0.04***
Age at child's birth 18–34 years	0.86	0.84	0.89	–0.05***
Age at child's birth >34 years	0.05	0.05	0.05	0.00
Completed formal education (years)	5.68	4.33	8.32	–3.98***
Employed	0.20	0.24	0.13	0.11***
Regularly exposed to mass media	0.85	0.81	0.93	–0.12***
Member of an NGO	0.15	0.18	0.09	0.10***
c. Household				
Standardized wealth index	–0.36	–0.72	0.34	–1.06***
Size	4.87	4.76	5.07	–0.31***
d. Neighborhood area				
Formal garbage collection available	0.69	0.62	0.84	–0.22***
Proper sewerage system available	0.48	0.41	0.62	–0.21***
CHW service available	0.51	0.55	0.44	0.10***
NGO health facility available	0.48	0.48	0.46	0.02
Public health facility available	0.14	0.14	0.14	–0.00
Pharmacy available	1.00	1.00	1.00	0.00
Other private health facility available	0.36	0.33	0.42	–0.09**

Source: Estimates based on 2013 Bangladesh Urban Health Survey data.
Note: The table reports estimated averages in columns (1), (2), and (3), and the difference in estimated averages between columns (2) and (3) appears in column (4). Estimates are adjusted for sampling weights. Inference is based on robust standard errors clustered at the neighborhood level. ARI = acute respiratory infection; CHW = community health worker; HAZ = height-for-age z-score; NGO = nongovernmental organization.
*$p < 0.10$; **$p < 0.05$; ***$p < 0.01$.

lower for slum children. Slum children were more likely to have mothers who were employed (24 percent versus 13 percent).

As for availability of health services and facilities, slum neighborhood areas were more likely than nonslum neighborhood areas to have CHWs (55 percent versus 44 percent) and less likely to have private health facilities (33 percent versus 42 percent). NGO and public health facilities as well as pharmacies were available at similar rates in slum and nonslum neighborhood areas.

Effects of Demographic and Socioeconomic Factors on Child HAZ

Table 3.3 reports the effects of various factors on HAZ, based on ordinary least squares regressions. Child age has a negative effect in all samples (full, slum,

Table 3.3 Effects on Under-Five Child HAZ in City Corporations, Base Set of Factors, 2013
Ordinary least squares regressions

Factor	Full (1)	Slum (2)	Nonslum (3)
Child			
Age	−0.015***	−0.017***	−0.013***
	(0.002)	(0.002)	(0.002)
Female	0.042	0.041	0.014
	(0.045)	(0.059)	(0.068)
Birth order	0.031	0.046	0.006
	(0.024)	(0.030)	(0.038)
Recently ill with fever or ARI symptoms	−0.019	0.031	−0.138*
	(0.052)	(0.069)	(0.071)
Mother			
Age at child's birth <18 years	−0.220***	−0.292***	0.036
	(0.085)	(0.104)	(0.133)
Age at child's birth >34 years	0.087	−0.143	0.525**
	(0.134)	(0.165)	(0.210)
Completed formal education (years)	0.034***	0.039***	0.022*
	(0.008)	(0.012)	(0.012)
Employed	−0.063	−0.045	−0.081
	(0.062)	(0.075)	(0.101)
Regularly exposed to mass media	0.108	0.073	0.247*
	(0.066)	(0.076)	(0.136)
Member of an NGO	0.081	0.173**	−0.195
	(0.072)	(0.083)	(0.122)
Household			
Standardized wealth index	0.213***	0.204***	0.244***
	(0.038)	(0.047)	(0.064)
Number of members	−0.021*	−0.017	−0.030
	(0.013)	(0.017)	(0.019)
Neighborhood area			
Formal garbage collection available	−0.016	−0.004	−0.082
	(0.069)	(0.083)	(0.119)
Proper sewerage system available	0.038	0.022	0.058
	(0.056)	(0.076)	(0.079)
CHW service available	−0.019	−0.018	−0.052
	(0.055)	(0.072)	(0.080)
NGO health facility available	−0.013	−0.068	0.090
	(0.059)	(0.075)	(0.079)
Public health facility available	−0.081	−0.015	−0.187*
	(0.079)	(0.103)	(0.110)
Private health facility available	0.091*	0.133*	0.048
	(0.053)	(0.070)	(0.077)

table continues next page

Table 3.3 Effects on Under-Five Child HAZ in City Corporations, Base Set of Factors, 2013 *(continued)*

Factor	Full (1)	Slum (2)	Nonslum (3)
Nonslum	0.202***	n.a.	n.a.
	(0.062)	n.a.	n.a.
Intercept	−1.576***	−1.567***	−1.365***
	(0.153)	(0.190)	(0.252)
Observations	7,565	5,000	2,565
R-squared statistic	0.082	0.064	0.064

Source: Estimates based on data from the 2013 Bangladesh Urban Health Survey.
Note: Regressions control for administrative divisions. Estimates are adjusted for sampling weights. Robust standard errors, clustered at the neighborhood-area level, are reported in parentheses. ARI = acute respiratory infection; CHW = community health worker; HAZ = height-for-age z-score; n.a. = not applicable; NGO = nongovernmental organization.
$*p < 0.10; **p < 0.05; ***p < 0.01.$

and nonslum). Child illness with fever or ARI symptoms has a significant negative effect in the nonslum sample. In the full sample, a child's birth when the mother was younger than 18 years of age has a significant negative effect compared with birth when the mother was aged 18–34 years. The full-sample effect is driven by the slum-sample effect.

Among the positive effects on child HAZ, mother's regular exposure to mass media has a significant positive effect in the nonslum sample. In the slum sample, a mother's membership in an NGO has a significant positive effect. Adams, Nababan, and Hanifi (2015) document the positive association between a mother's NGO membership and the use of reproductive, maternal, newborn, and child health (RMNCH) services. The observed effect of NGO membership on child HAZ may be mediated by the use of RMNCH services, which are not controlled for in the regressions.

In all samples, the mother's education attainment and household wealth have significant positive effects on child HAZ. In the full sample, an additional year of mother's education has a positive effect of 0.034 SD, and a 1 SD increase in household wealth (that is, going from the average to the 84th percentile in the index) has a positive effect of 0.213 SD. Household size has a negative effect in both the slum and nonslum samples, but only the full-sample effect of –0.021 SD is significant.

As for availability of health services and facilities, the presence of CHWs and NGO and public health facilities in the neighborhood area has negative but mostly insignificant effects on child HAZ. The exception is the nonslum-sample effect of the availability of public health facilities, which is a significant –0.187 SD. The negative effects are likely placement effects: that is, areas served by CHWs and NGO and public health facilities may be socioeconomically disadvantaged in ways not fully reflected by household wealth and neighborhood-area environmental quality factors included in the regressions. Simply residing in a nonslum neighborhood area has a significant positive effect of 0.202 SD.

In all samples—full, slum, or nonslum—factors such as the child's gender or birth order, the mother's employment status, and the availability of formal garbage collection and a proper sewerage system in the neighborhood area have insignificant effects.

Ahsan and others (2017) examined the effects of various factors on stunting and underweight status for slum and nonslum children using 2013 BUHS data as well. They found that the child's age, mother's education attainment, and household wealth are significant factors for slum and nonslum children, and that mother's membership in an NGO and the child's birth order are additional significant factors for nonslum children. For factors that are similar between this study's analysis and Ahsan and others (2017), inference results from the study's regressions for slum and nonslum samples match those from their final stunting regression specifications.

This study's findings are also largely consistent with those from studies of the determinants of child undernutrition in selected slum settlements in various urban centers in Bangladesh (Alam and others 2011; Fakir and Khan 2015; Zaman and others 2015), as well as with international evidence on the determinants of child undernutrition in slum areas (Abuya, Ciera, and Kimani-Murage 2012; Goudet and others 2017).

Effects of Maternal and Child Health Service Use on Child HAZ

The analysis examines the effects on HAZ of child antenatal care, delivery, and newborn exam performed at health facilities. The information on child antenatal care, delivery, and newborn exam were gathered in the survey only for the youngest child born in the three years before the survey (61 percent of the study's full analysis sample).

Average Levels of Health Service Use

Table 3.4 reports the rates of health service use, by provider type. In the full sample, mothers of 70 percent of children received antenatal care in a health facility, 49 percent of children were delivered in a health facility, and 40 percent of children received a newborn exam in a health facility. Although there are cases of antenatal care and newborn exam by qualified health professionals at home, the shares are in the low single digits; these cases are combined with no service.

The use of private providers and facilities dominates. Mothers of 31 percent of children received antenatal care at a private health facility, 23 percent at an NGO health facility, and 16 percent at a public health facility. Similarly, 21 percent of children were delivered at a private health facility, and 14 percent each at NGO and public health facilities. Eighteen percent of children had a newborn exam at a private health facility, and 11 percent each at NGO and public health facilities.

Rates of health service use are poorer for slum children than nonslum children. The rates of antenatal care, delivery, and newborn exam in any health facility are 22–25 percentage points lower for slum children. However, use of NGO

Table 3.4 Average Use of Maternal and Child Health Services in City Corporations, by Provider and Neighborhood-Area Type, 2013

Indicator	Full (1)	Slum (2)	Nonslum (3)	Slum-nonslum (4)
a. Antenatal care				
Any health facility	0.70	0.62	0.86	−0.24***
Public health facility	0.16	0.14	0.18	−0.04**
NGO health facility	0.23	0.27	0.17	0.10***
Private health facility	0.31	0.21	0.52	−0.31***
b. Delivery				
Any health facility	0.49	0.41	0.66	−0.25***
Public health facility	0.14	0.12	0.17	−0.05***
NGO health facility	0.14	0.17	0.09	0.08***
Private health facility	0.21	0.12	0.40	−0.28***
c. Newborn exam				
Any health facility	0.40	0.33	0.55	−0.22***
Public health facility	0.11	0.10	0.15	−0.05***
NGO health facility	0.11	0.13	0.07	0.06***
Private health facility	0.18	0.11	0.33	−0.23***

Source: Estimates based on data from the 2013 Bangladesh Urban Health Survey.
Note: The sample comprises the youngest child born to a mother in the preceding three years. The table reports estimated averages in columns (1), (2), and (3), and the difference in estimated averages between columns (2) and (3) appears in column (4). Estimates are adjusted for sampling weights. Inference is based on robust standard errors clustered at the neighborhood-area level. NGO = nongovernmental organization.
*$p < 0.10$; **$p < 0.05$; ***$p < 0.01$.

health facilities for these services is higher for slum children, and use of private health facilities lower. For example, mothers of 27 percent of slum children received antenatal care from an NGO health facility, compared with 17 percent in the case of nonslum children; and mothers of 21 percent of slum children received such care from a private health facility, compared with 52 percent in the case of nonslum children.

The survey also asked mothers why they chose a given delivery site for the youngest child born in the three years before the survey (table 3.5). In the full sample, the main reason that the mother chose to deliver in a health facility was due to pregnancy or delivery complications (55 percent of cases), followed by safety of the health facility (29 percent of cases). In addition, the main reason that the mother chose the *specific* health facility was safety (33 percent of cases), followed by prior knowledge about the provider or receipt of antenatal care there (17 percent of cases each). Mothers reported cost to be the reason for the choice of the specific health facility in 6 percent of cases, and proximity of the health facility to home in 10 percent of cases. For children who were delivered at home, mothers predominantly reported that they felt it was not necessary to deliver at a health facility (70 percent of cases). Cost or lack of money was reported for only 12 percent of cases.

Table 3.5 Reported Reasons for Mother's Choice of Delivery Location in City Corporations, by Neighborhood-Area Type, 2013

Indicator	Full (1)	Slum (2)	Nonslum (3)	Slum-nonslum (4)
a. Why chose a facility for delivery				
Due to complications	0.55	0.56	0.54	0.02
Referred by doctor/service provider	0.09	0.09	0.08	0.00
It is safe	0.29	0.29	0.29	−0.01
Other (unspecified)	0.07	0.07	0.08	−0.02
b. Why chose specific facility for delivery				
Low cost	0.06	0.09	0.04	0.05***
Near to my house	0.10	0.11	0.07	0.04**
It is safe	0.33	0.32	0.34	−0.02
Provider is known	0.17	0.14	0.21	−0.06***
Had antenatal care here	0.14	0.13	0.15	−0.01
Had previous delivery here	0.03	0.02	0.04	−0.03***
Other (unspecified)	0.17	0.18	0.15	0.03
c. Why chose delivery at home				
Not necessary	0.70	0.70	0.71	−0.01
Costs too much/lack of money	0.12	0.13	0.09	0.04**
Better care at home	0.05	0.05	0.06	−0.01
Other (unspecified)	0.13	0.12	0.14	−0.02

Source: Estimates based on data from the 2013 Bangladesh Urban Health Survey.
Note: The sample for panels a and b is youngest child born in a health facility in the three years before the survey; the sample for panel c is youngest child born at home in the three years before the survey. The table reports estimated averages in columns (1), (2), and (3), and the difference in estimated averages between columns (2) and (3) appears in column (4). Estimates are adjusted for sampling weights. Inference is based on robust standard errors clustered at the neighborhood-area level.
*p < 0.10; **p < 0.05; ***p < 0.01.

Slum mothers were more likely than nonslum mothers to report cost or distance as the reasons for their choice of the specific health facility. (Cost was cited by 9 percent of slum mothers versus 4 percent of nonslum mothers. Distance was cited by 11 percent and 7 percent, respectively). Among those who delivered at home, slum mothers were also more likely than nonslum mothers to report cost or lack of money to be the reason for their choice (13 percent and 9 percent, respectively).

Effects of Health Service Use

The type of health facility for antenatal care or delivery may influence child HAZ if, for example, the type of health facility is associated with quality of care. Mothers may choose to receive antenatal care or to deliver at a specific type of health facility because they expect to obtain better care there for any pregnancy or delivery complications. Even if they obtain better care, however, complications may induce a negative association between a higher-quality health facility or provider type and child HAZ.

Table 3.6 reports the effects on child HAZ of the use of various maternal and child health services at a health facility in general (panel a) and at specific types of health facility (panel b), based on regression. The regressions control for other factors—notably for household wealth, which could influence (a) whether households use free or subsidized public or NGO health services or, alternatively, fee-based private health services; and (b) the availability of RMNCH services in the neighborhood area through CHWs and health facilities.

Table 3.6 Effects on Under-Five Child HAZ of Health Facility Use for Antenatal Care, Delivery, and Newborn Exam in City Corporations, by Neighborhood-Area Type, 2013
Ordinary least squares regressions

Factor	Full (1)	Slum (2)	Nonslum (3)
a. Use of any health facility			
Antenatal care at a health facility	0.182**	0.158	0.256*
	(0.090)	(0.107)	(0.136)
Delivery at a health facility	0.022	−0.022	0.037
	(0.114)	(0.149)	(0.174)
Newborn exam at a health facility	0.008	0.056	−0.025
	(0.114)	(0.158)	(0.152)
b. Use of health facility type			
Antenatal care			
Public health facility	0.171	0.018	0.466**
	(0.128)	(0.159)	(0.191)
NGO health facility	0.176*	0.233*	0.054
	(0.105)	(0.126)	(0.157)
Private health facility	0.206*	0.196	0.267*
Delivery			
Public health facility	0.001	−0.012	−0.031
	(0.192)	(0.275)	(0.218)
NGO health facility	−0.014	0.034	−0.193
	(0.150)	(0.184)	(0.242)
Private health facility	0.091	−0.109	0.202
	(0.172)	(0.261)	(0.231)
Newborn exam			
Public health facility	0.244	0.306	0.145
	(0.201)	(0.293)	(0.212)
NGO health facility	−0.083	−0.159	0.156
	(0.169)	(0.206)	(0.247)
Private health facility	−0.116	0.070	−0.221
	(0.173)	(0.277)	(0.215)

Source: Estimates based on data from the 2013 Bangladesh Urban Health Survey.
Note: Regressions control for the base set of factors (see table 3.3) and administrative divisions. Estimates are adjusted for sampling weights. Robust standard errors, clustered at the neighborhood level, are reported in parentheses. HAZ = height-for-age z-score; NGO = nongovernmental organization.
*p < 0.10; **p < 0.05; ***p < 0.01.

Antenatal care at a health facility has a significant positive effect of 0.182 SD in the full sample. The slum-sample effect of 0.158 SD is insignificant, whereas the nonslum-sample effect of 0.256 SD is significant. The effects of delivery or newborn exam in a health facility are insignificant for all samples.

Looking by type of health facility, antenatal care in a public health facility has a significant effect of 0.466 SD in the nonslum sample; antenatal care in an NGO health facility has a significant positive effect of 0.233 SD in the slum sample; and antenatal care in a private health facility has positive effects of 0.196 SD in the slum sample and 0.267 SD in the nonslum sample, but only the latter effect is significant. The effects of delivery and newborn exam by facility type are insignificant in all samples.

Effects of Health-Protective Household Amenities on Child HAZ

A sanitary community and home environment can protect children from illness, and thereby promote nutrition status. Reviews of international evidence suggest that poor water, sanitation, and hygiene (WASH) facilities and practices are significantly associated with child diarrhea and intestinal parasitic infection (Clasen and others 2007; Fewtrell and others 2005; Strunz and others 2014; Ziegelbauer and others 2012), and that diarrhea is significantly associated with poorer nutrition status (Dewey and Mayers 2011). The international evaluative evidence also generally suggests that improved WASH has a positive, albeit modest, effect on child growth (Dangour and others 2013). While much more limited, evidence from other countries suggests a negative link between indoor air pollution and nutrition status (Mishra and Retherford 2007) and a positive link between built home flooring and health and nutrition status (Cattaneo and others 2009).

In terms of evidence for Bangladesh, Luby and Halder (2008) found that a handwashing place at the dwelling is significantly associated with a lower rate of ARI symptoms among young children in a sample of households in Dhaka city. Lin and others (2013) found that sanitary household WASH conditions were significantly associated with a lower rate of intestinal parasitic infection, better nutrition status, and lower rates of markers of environmental enteropathy among young children in a sample of rural households. Baker and others (2016) found that young children in households that share toilet facilities have a significantly higher rate of diarrhea in Mirzapur city (as well as in selected urban centers in Africa and other South Asian countries).

Motivated by this evidence, the study examines the effects of household access to piped drinking water and an improved toilet, safe disposal of garbage by the household, household use of a clean fuel for cooking, a finished floor in the dwelling, and a handwashing site with soap and water at the dwelling.

Average Levels of Health-Protective Household Amenities

Table 3.7 reports average levels for potential health-protective household amenities, as follows:

- *Piped drinking water:* Forty-five percent of children belonged to households with shared access to piped drinking water, whereas another 19 percent belonged to households with unshared access.
- *Access to improved toilet:* Virtually all children belonged to households with access to an improved toilet, but shared access was common. Thirty-one percent belonged to households with unshared access, whereas 37 percent shared access with up to 10 households, and 31 percent shared access with more than 10 households.
- *Safe garbage disposal:* Fifty-three percent of children belonged to households that safely disposed of household garbage (through collection or by disposal in an outside bin).
- *Clean cooking fuel:* Seventy-one percent of children belonged to households that used a clean cooking fuel (liquid petroleum gas, natural gas, kerosene, or biogas).
- *Built (nonearth) floor:* Eight-four percent of children resided in a dwelling with a built floor.
- *Handwashing site on premises:* Forty-five percent of children belonged to households that had a handwashing site on the premises with water and soap.

Table 3.7 Average Levels of Health-Protective Household Amenities for Under-Five Children in City Corporations, by Neighborhood-Area Type, 2013

Factor	Full (1)	Slum (2)	Nonslum (3)	Slum-nonslum (4)
No access to piped drinking water	0.36	0.44	0.22	0.21***
Unshared access to piped drinking water	0.19	0.05	0.47	−0.43***
Shared access to piped drinking water	0.45	0.52	0.31	0.21***
Access to improved toilet, unshared	0.31	0.14	0.62	−0.48***
Access to improved toilet, shared with 1–10 HH	0.37	0.41	0.30	0.11***
Access to improved toilet, shared with >10 HH	0.31	0.42	0.08	0.35***
Safe disposal of garbage	0.53	0.45	0.68	−0.23***
Use of clean cooking fuel	0.71	0.64	0.87	−0.23***
Nonearth floor in dwelling	0.84	0.78	0.95	−0.17***
Handwashing site, with water and soap, at dwelling	0.45	0.29	0.74	−0.45***

Source: Estimates based on data from the 2013 Bangladesh Urban Health Survey.
Note: The table reports estimated averages in columns (1), (2), and (3), and the difference in estimated averages between columns (2) and (3) appears in column (4). Estimates are adjusted for sampling weights. Inference is based on robust standard errors clustered at the neighborhood-area level. HH = households.
*$p < 0.10$; **$p < 0.05$; ***$p < 0.01$.

Access to and availability of these household amenities were significantly poorer for slum children than nonslum children. For example, slum children were much more likely than nonslum children to belong to households that share access to an improved toilet: 42 percent of slum children shared access to an improved toilet with more than 10 households, compared with 8 percent of nonslum children.

Effects of Health-Protective Household Amenities

Table 3.8 reports the effects of potential health-protective household amenities on child HAZ. Given that virtually all households had access to improved toilets, the analysis is restricted to children in such households and examines the effect of shared access to an improved toilet. The amenities are strongly correlated with the household wealth index, even when they are excluded from the construction of the index. Thus, the effects of the amenities are examined, controlling for other factors but excluding the household wealth index.

In the full sample, sharing access to an improved toilet with more than 10 households has a significant negative effect (–0.202 SD) on child HAZ. This effect is driven by the slum-sample effect (–0.272 SD). Sharing access to an

Table 3.8 Effects of Health-Protective Household Amenities on Under-Five Child HAZ in City Corporations, by Neighborhood-Area Type, 2013

Ordinary least squares regressions

Factor	Full (1)	Slum (2)	Nonslum (3)
Unshared access to piped drinking water	0.118	–0.016	0.102
	(0.108)	(0.170)	(0.146)
Shared access to piped drinking water	0.066	0.098	–0.044
	(0.064)	(0.076)	(0.116)
Access to an improved toilet, shared with 1–10 HH	–0.101	–0.130	–0.034
	(0.093)	(0.131)	(0.128)
Access to an improved toilet, shared with >10 HH	–0.202*	–0.272**	0.025
	(0.103)	(0.133)	(0.174)
Safe disposal of garbage	0.085	0.081	0.116
	(0.062)	(0.078)	(0.093)
Use of a clean cooking fuel	–0.002	–0.043	0.203
	(0.081)	(0.092)	(0.169)
Nonearth floor in dwelling	0.061	0.102	–0.019
	(0.082)	(0.089)	(0.190)
Handwashing site, with water and soap, at dwelling	0.095	0.040	0.239**
	(0.061)	(0.076)	(0.095)

Source: Estimates based on data from the 2013 Bangladesh Urban Health Survey.
Note: Sample is restricted to children in households with access to an improved toilet. Regressions control for the base set of factors, except for the household wealth index (see table 3.3); they also control for administrative divisions. Estimates are adjusted for sampling weights. Robust standard errors, clustered at the neighborhood-area level, are reported in parentheses. HAZ = height-for-age z-score; HH = households.
*$p < 0.10$; **$p < 0.05$; ***$p < 0.01$.

improved toilet with fewer households also has negative effects in all samples, but they are insignificant. Having a handwashing site in the dwelling with soap and water has a significant positive effect of 0.24 SD for nonslum children. The corresponding effect for slum children is 0.04 SD and insignificant. All other amenities have insignificant effects.

As a caveat, the study's analysis of the effects of household amenities does not account for the quality, reliability, or time availability of these amenities. Large-scale evidence on these dimensions is lacking for Bangladesh. The study's finding that households that share toilets with several other households have lower child HAZ may be because these communal toilets are particularly unclean and poorly maintained (Alam and others 2016).

Effects of Mother Moving to a City Corporation on Child HAZ

Evidence is highly limited, and mixed, on the effects of within-country rural-urban migration on health and nutrition outcomes in low- and middle-income countries (Mu and de Brauw 2015). The study examines the effect on child HAZ of such migration by mothers in three dimensions: (a) the type of location from which the mother moved (from another urban center or from a rural area); (b) the mother's reported reason for moving to the current city corporation (work-related, family-related, or "other" such as education- or property-related); and (c) the number of years since the mother moved to the current city corporation.

Separate questions to the mother concerned whether the move to the current city corporation was due to loss from an adverse natural event (salinity, flood, cyclone, drought, or river erosion) or whether any move in the past was due to an adverse natural event. Less than 1 percent of mothers reported adverse natural events as the reason for moving.

Average Levels of Migration-Related Factors

Table 3.9 reports summary statistics for the various dimensions of the mother's move decision. In the full sample, 12 percent of children had mothers who were born in an urban center other than the current city corporation, and 54 percent had mothers who were born in a rural area. Conditional on moving to the current city corporation, 67 percent of children had mothers who had moved for family reasons, 29 percent for work reasons, and 4 percent for other reasons. Average years since the move was 8.52 years.

Slum children were more likely than nonslum children to have mothers who were born in a rural area (57 percent and 49 percent, respectively). Slum children were also more likely than nonslum children to have mothers who had moved to the city corporation for work-related reasons (33 percent and 20 percent, respectively). The average number of years since the mother's move were similar for slum and nonslum children.

Effects of Mother's Migration

Conceivably, various mechanisms could generate positive or negative effects on child HAZ due to a mother's moving to the current city corporation, the reason

Table 3.9 Average Levels for Mother's Migration to Current City Corporation for Under-Five Children in City Corporations, by Neighborhood-Area Type, 2013

Factor	Full (1)	Slum (2)	Nonslum (3)	Slum-nonslum (4)
a. Mother's birth location				
Born in another urban center[a]	0.12	0.11	0.13	−0.02*
Born in a rural area	0.54	0.57	0.49	0.08***
b. Reason for move[b]				
Family reasons	0.67	0.63	0.74	−0.11***
Work reasons	0.29	0.33	0.20	0.13***
Other reasons	0.04	0.04	0.06	−0.02**
c. Time since mother's move[b]				
Years since move[c]	8.52	8.60	8.37	0.22

Source: Estimates based on data from the 2013 Bangladesh Urban Health Survey.
Note: The table reports estimated averages in columns (1), (2), and (3), and the difference in estimated averages between columns (2) and (3) appears in column (4). Estimates are adjusted for sampling weights. Inference is based on robust standard errors clustered at the neighborhood-area level.
a. "Another urban center" is any urban entity other than the current city corporation.
b. Panels b and c report statistics conditional on the mother having moved to the current city corporation.
c. A mother who had moved to the current city corporation just before the survey was assigned a time since the move of one month.
*p < 0.10; **p < 0.05; ***p < 0.01.

for the move, or the number of years residing in the current city corporation, depending on whether the upside or downside risks to health and nutrition from living in an urban area dominate. Thus, the net effect on child nutrition status of a mother's move to the current city corporation is theoretically ambiguous.

Table 3.10 reports the effects on child HAZ of the mother moving to the current city corporation, controlling for the base set of factors. The reference category for the effect of birth location is "mother born in the current city corporation." The reference category for the effect of reason for move is "mother always resided in the current city corporation." Mothers who moved for reasons other than work or family are omitted from the regressions. The regressions for the effect of time since the mother's move is conditional on moving to the current city corporation.

Mother born in another urban center has a significant positive effect (0.181 SD) in the full sample.[4] The full-sample effect is driven by the slum-sample effect (0.252 SD). Mother born in a rural area has a significant positive effect (0.140 SD) in the nonslum sample. Mother moving for work reasons has a significant positive effect (0.298 SD) in the nonslum sample. Time since the mother moved has positive, but insignificant, effects in all samples. Discretizing years since the mother moved to the current city corporation, Ahsan and others (2017) also find that this factor has no significant effect on child stunting status in either their slum or nonslum regressions. At the very least, the collective evidence suggests that a mother's migration to the current city corporation, whether to a slum or nonslum neighborhood area, does not appear to have a negative effect on child HAZ.

Table 3.10 Effects of Mother's Migration to Current City Corporation on Under-Five Child HAZ in City Corporations, by Neighborhood-Area Type, 2013

Ordinary least squares regressions

Factor	Full (1)	Slum (2)	Nonslum (3)
a. Mother's birth location[a]			
Born in another urban center[b]	0.181**	0.252**	0.064
	(0.084)	(0.110)	(0.122)
Born in a rural area	0.054	0.016	0.140*
	(0.054)	(0.071)	(0.078)
b. Reason for move[c]			
Family reasons	0.024	0.018	0.056
	(0.057)	(0.077)	(0.079)
Work reasons	0.051	−0.016	0.298***
	(0.074)	(0.090)	(0.113)
c. Time since mother's move			
Time since move (years)[d]	0.006	0.007	0.002
	(0.005)	(0.007)	(0.008)

Source: Estimates based on data from the 2013 Bangladesh Urban Health Survey.
Note: Regressions control for the base set of factors (see table 3.3) and administrative divisions. Estimates are adjusted for sampling weights. Robust standard errors, clustered at the neighborhood-area level, are reported in parentheses. HAZ = height-for-age z-score.
a. The reference category is "mother born in the current city corporation."
b. "Another urban center" is any urban entity other than the current city corporation.
c. The reference category is "mother always resided in the current city corporation."
d. A mother who had moved to the current city corporation just before the survey was assigned a time since the move of one month.
*p < 0.10; **p < 0.05; ***p < 0.01.

In related research, Islam and Gagnon (2016) use 2006 BUHS data to examine the effects of a mother's migration on the use of RMNCH services. Specifically, the authors look at the effects of whether the mother moved to a city corporation and, for migrant mothers, how long the mother had resided in the current city corporation, whether she was born in a rural area, and whether she self-reported moving for employment or education reasons. They find that a mother's migration has significant negative effects on the use of various maternal and child health services, while years lived in the current city corporation has a positive effect only on the use of antenatal care services. Given these findings, the study reestimates the effects of the various measures related to the mother moving to the current city corporation, controlling for the use of maternal and child health services in the relevant child subsamples. The results generally continue to hold.

Adult Health and Nutrition Outcomes

We next report findings from examining health and nutrition outcomes for women and men in city corporations, based on the 2006 BUHS. As noted in chapter 2, we use the 2006 BUHS because similar outcome information was not collected in the 2013 BUHS.

Average Levels of Adult Health and Nutrition Status

With respect to women, the study finds the following average health and nutrition outcomes in the full sample (table 3.11): 16 percent reported being unhealthy, 20 percent had a serious illness, 6 percent had a serious injury, and 20 percent had physical difficulty with routine activities. Nineteen percent were underweight, 25 percent were overweight, 12 percent had diabetes, and 28 percent had hypertension.

Slum women had higher rates of illness and difficulty with physical mobility than nonslum women. Slum women also were shorter, had higher mental ill-health scores, and were more likely to be underweight than nonslum women. Conversely, nonslum women were more likely than slum women to be overweight and have hypertension and diabetes. The only health outcome without a significant difference in averages between slum and nonslum women was the rate of injury.

With respect to men, the study finds the following average health and nutrition outcomes in the full sample (table 3.12): 9 percent reported being unhealthy, 16 percent had a serious illness, 8 percent had a serious injury, and 19 percent had physical difficulty with routine activities. Twenty-six percent were underweight, 13 percent were overweight, 10 percent had diabetes, and 17 percent had hypertension. Men had better outcomes than women regarding mental ill-health, hypertension, and overweight status, while men had a worse outcome than women regarding underweight status.

Table 3.11 Average Levels of Women's Health and Nutrition Status in City Corporations, by Neighborhood-Area Type, 2006

Indicator	Full (1)	Slum (2)	Nonslum (3)	Slum-nonslum (4)
Self-reported to be unhealthy	0.16	0.19	0.12	0.06***
Serious illness	0.20	0.22	0.18	0.04***
Serious injury	0.06	0.06	0.06	0.00
Difficulty with mobility	0.20	0.22	0.18	0.04***
Log mental ill-health score[a]	1.31	1.39	1.21	0.18**
Height (centimeters)	150.76	150.13	151.33	−1.20***
Underweight	0.19	0.26	0.12	0.14***
Overweight	0.25	0.15	0.34	−0.19***
Diabetes	0.12	0.05	0.17	−0.12***
Hypertension	0.28	0.23	0.32	−0.09*

Source: Estimates based on data from the 2006 Bangladesh Urban Health Survey.
Note: The table reports estimated averages in columns (1), (2), and (3), and the difference in estimated averages between columns (2) and (3) appears in column (4). Estimates are adjusted for survey sampling weights. Inference for the difference in estimated averages is based on robust p-values clustered at the level of the primary sampling unit. Health and nutrition variables for which regressions are run are italicized.
a. As further discussed in chapter 2, the mental health measure was specially constructed from 20 depression- and anxiety-related questions in the World Health Organization's Self-Reporting Questionnaire (SRQ20). Mental ill-health scores as a continuous variable are used here, logging values to reduce the degree of right skewness in the outcome distribution (zeros were set to 0.1 before the log transformation).
*$p < 0.10$; **$p < 0.05$; ***$p < 0.01$.

Table 3.12 Average Levels of Men's Health and Nutrition Status in City Corporations, by Neighborhood-Area Type, 2006

Indicator	Full (1)	Slum (2)	Nonslum (3)	Slum-nonslum (4)
Self-reported to be unhealthy	0.09	0.11	0.07	0.04***
Serious illness	0.16	0.19	0.13	0.06***
Serious injury	0.08	0.09	0.07	0.02**
Difficulty with mobility	0.19	0.23	0.15	0.08***
Log mental ill-health score[a]	0.73	0.85	0.59	0.26**
Height (centimeters)	163.35	162.10	164.33	−2.23***
Underweight	0.26	0.35	0.19	0.16***
Overweight	0.13	0.07	0.18	−0.11***
Diabetes	0.10	0.07	0.12	−0.04
Hypertension	0.17	0.15	0.18	−0.03

Source: Estimates based on data from the 2006 Bangladesh Urban Health Survey.
Note: This table reports estimated averages in columns (1), (2), and (3), and the difference in estimated averages between columns (2) and (3) in column (4). Estimates are adjusted for survey sampling weights. Inference for the difference in estimated averages is based on robust *p*-values clustered at the level of the primary sampling unit. Health and nutrition variables for which regressions are run are italicized.
a. As discussed further in chapter 2, the mental health measure was specially constructed, derived from 20 questions in the World Health Organization's Self-Reporting Questionnaire (SRQ20). Mental ill-health scores as a continuous variable are used here, logging values to reduce the degree of right skewness in the outcome distribution (zeros were set to 0.1 before the log transformation).
p < 0.10; **p* < 0.05; ***p* < 0.01.

In general, the patterns in differences in averages between slum and non-slum men mirror those for women. However, in contrast to the patterns for women, the injury rate was higher for slum men than nonslum men, and the rates of diabetes and hypertension were similar between slum men and nonslum men.

Effects of Individual, Household, and Neighborhood-Area Factors
Tables 3.13 and 3.14 report the regression results for women and men, respectively. All tables are structured similarly. Regression results are reported separately by outcome and sample (full, slum, and nonslum). Given that the outcomes are binary, odds ratios are reported.

Individual Factors
In general (across the full sample), age is negatively associated with the likelihood of underweight status; it is also positively associated with the likelihood of overweight status as well as with mental ill-health scores for both women and men. Relative to no formal schooling, completing 10 years or more of schooling is also associated with a lower likelihood of underweight status and a higher likelihood of overweight status, but with lower mental ill-health scores for both men and women. (However, only 16 percent of women and 22 percent of men had completed at least 10 years of schooling.)

Migration- and employment-related factors were also associated with certain health and nutrition outcomes. Relative to always residing in the current

Table 3.13 Correlates of Underweight, Overweight, and Mental Ill-Health Status in Women, City Corporations, 2006

Ever-married females, aged 18–49 years

	Underweight[a]			Overweight[b]			Log mental ill-health scores[c]		
	Full	Slum	Nonslum	Full	Slum	Nonslum	Full	Slum	Nonslum
Factor	(1)	(2)	(3)	(4)	(5)	(6)	(7)	(8)	(9)
Age	0.973***	0.986*	0.948***	1.059***	1.068***	1.054***	0.021***	0.025***	0.016***
	(0.008)	(0.008)	(0.016)	(0.010)	(0.011)	(0.016)	(0.003)	(0.002)	(0.006)
Highest ed.: preschool–grade 4	0.787	0.965	0.505*	1.483**	1.124	1.870**	-0.007	0.070	-0.132
	(0.127)	(0.164)	(0.184)	(0.262)	(0.231)	(0.503)	(0.077)	(0.075)	(0.176)
Highest ed.: grades 5–7	0.732*	0.856	0.513*	1.947***	1.840***	2.162***	-0.025	-0.089	0.056
	(0.128)	(0.154)	(0.197)	(0.316)	(0.291)	(0.615)	(0.069)	(0.066)	(0.142)
Highest ed.: grades 8–9	1.093	1.128	0.908	1.571*	1.615*	1.650	-0.101	-0.048	-0.126
	(0.203)	(0.264)	(0.301)	(0.366)	(0.409)	(0.580)	(0.080)	(0.107)	(0.134)
Highest ed.: grades 10–11	0.865	0.679	0.819	1.666**	1.603	1.773*	-0.349***	-0.332**	-0.376**
	(0.270)	(0.281)	(0.377)	(0.393)	(0.523)	(0.579)	(0.110)	(0.128)	(0.156)
Highest ed.: grade 12 or higher	0.274***	0.861	0.153***	1.793*	2.530***	1.838	-0.522***	-0.559***	-0.552***
	(0.109)	(0.492)	(0.072)	(0.540)	(1.062)	(0.708)	(0.097)	(0.181)	(0.131)
Moved to current neighborhood area	1.061	0.952	1.136	0.699***	0.722**	0.689**	-0.021	-0.078*	0.034
	(0.141)	(0.127)	(0.340)	(0.075)	(0.104)	(0.103)	(0.051)	(0.041)	(0.093)
Employed	1.159	1.088	1.276	0.658***	0.606***	0.686	0.126***	0.081	0.219**
	(0.140)	(0.144)	(0.313)	(0.096)	(0.102)	(0.158)	(0.048)	(0.053)	(0.086)
Own/joint hdm authority score[d]	0.899*	0.867**	0.985	0.999	0.943	1.037	-0.059***	-0.029	-0.098***
	(0.050)	(0.049)	(0.112)	(0.054)	(0.060)	(0.082)	(0.019)	(0.022)	(0.034)
Log mental ill-health score[c]	1.204***	1.118*	1.371**	0.916**	0.982	0.889**	n.a.	n.a.	n.a.
	(0.068)	(0.066)	(0.166)	(0.040)	(0.057)	(0.053)			
Household size	0.988	0.991	0.982	1.055*	1.028	1.068	-0.032**	-0.014	-0.052**
	(0.030)	(0.033)	(0.059)	(0.032)	(0.037)	(0.048)	(0.014)	(0.013)	(0.022)

table continues next page

Table 3.13 Correlates of Underweight, Overweight, and Mental Ill-Health Status in Women, City Corporations, 2006 (continued)

Factor	Underweight[a]			Overweight[b]			Log mental ill-health scores[c]		
	Full (1)	Slum (2)	Nonslum (3)	Full (4)	Slum (5)	Nonslum (6)	Full (7)	Slum (8)	Nonslum (9)
Housing space per member	0.986 (0.024)	0.931** (0.032)	1.024 (0.020)	1.008 (0.011)	1.036 (0.023)	1.005 (0.012)	-0.007** (0.004)	-0.006 (0.005)	-0.007 (0.005)
Housing quality index[e]	0.800*** (0.062)	0.841** (0.064)	0.724 (0.146)	1.397*** (0.105)	1.496*** (0.109)	1.319** (0.164)	-0.077** (0.031)	-0.095*** (0.034)	-0.049 (0.055)
Household faced food shortage	1.166 (0.203)	1.396** (0.224)	0.617 (0.372)	1.148 (0.425)	0.840 (0.297)	1.884 (1.370)	0.455*** (0.063)	0.376*** (0.061)	0.682*** (0.142)
Log per-member hh con expenditures	0.556*** (0.066)	0.683** (0.101)	0.410*** (0.071)	2.429*** (0.319)	1.986*** (0.293)	2.610*** (0.487)	0.007 (0.055)	-0.006 (0.050)	0.028 (0.091)
Neighborhood-area environmental quality index[f]	0.986 (0.061)	0.955 (0.065)	0.892 (0.139)	1.009 (0.050)	1.036 (0.063)	0.897 (0.085)	0.003 (0.033)	-0.003 (0.033)	0.048 (0.097)
Pharmacy in neighborhood area	0.995 (0.122)	1.091 (0.167)	0.777 (0.150)	0.846* (0.075)	1.034 (0.135)	0.723*** (0.082)	0.033 (0.094)	0.095 (0.114)	-0.141 (0.139)
Qualified doctor in neighborhood area	0.999 (0.105)	1.039 (0.137)	0.905 (0.154)	1.169* (0.100)	0.962 (0.125)	1.366*** (0.150)	0.022 (0.094)	-0.035 (0.130)	0.081 (0.113)
CHW service in neighborhood area	0.936 (0.110)	1.038 (0.146)	0.735 (0.160)	0.933 (0.099)	0.990 (0.144)	0.901 (0.147)	-0.059 (0.082)	0.058 (0.092)	-0.200 (0.134)
Public health facility in neighborhood area	1.130 (0.316)	1.026 (0.365)	1.554 (0.583)	1.222 (0.178)	1.343* (0.217)	1.240 (0.309)	-0.003 (0.103)	0.093 (0.172)	-0.127 (0.108)
Private health facility in neighborhood area	1.053 (0.142)	1.118 (0.151)	0.949 (0.286)	1.007 (0.076)	1.043 (0.128)	1.052 (0.115)	0.186*** (0.068)	0.120 (0.087)	0.319*** (0.099)
NGO health facility in neighborhood area	0.718*** (0.078)	0.734** (0.087)	0.686* (0.149)	1.266*** (0.098)	1.245* (0.140)	1.263** (0.137)	0.047 (0.090)	0.034 (0.106)	0.108 (0.117)

table continues next page

Table 3.13 Correlates of Underweight, Overweight, and Mental Ill-Health Status in Women, City Corporations, 2006 (continued)

Factor	Underweight[a] Full (1)	Underweight[a] Slum (2)	Underweight[a] Nonslum (3)	Overweight[b] Full (4)	Overweight[b] Slum (5)	Overweight[b] Nonslum (6)	Log mental ill-health scores[c] Full (7)	Log mental ill-health scores[c] Slum (8)	Log mental ill-health scores[c] Nonslum (9)
Nonslum neighborhood area	0.669***	n.a.	n.a.	1.141	n.a.	n.a.	-0.028	n.a.	n.a.
	(0.094)	n.a.	n.a.	(0.116)	n.a.	n.a.	(0.078)	n.a.	n.a.
Barisal	1.147	0.899	0.939	0.835	0.938	0.802	0.168*	-0.010	0.349**
	(0.236)	(0.196)	(0.399)	(0.218)	(0.373)	(0.311)	(0.101)	(0.118)	(0.166)
Chittagong	0.992	1.088	0.997	1.124	1.070	1.199	0.112	0.195**	0.050
	(0.123)	(0.160)	(0.216)	(0.100)	(0.147)	(0.133)	(0.077)	(0.088)	(0.130)
Khulna	0.694	0.790	0.576	1.262	1.202	1.249	0.370***	0.280***	0.448***
	(0.155)	(0.222)	(0.224)	(0.211)	(0.290)	(0.272)	(0.062)	(0.080)	(0.095)
Rajshahi	0.926	0.910	0.909	0.898	1.207	0.778	-0.182	-0.071	-0.313
	(0.172)	(0.262)	(0.259)	(0.214)	(0.272)	(0.204)	(0.124)	(0.092)	(0.237)
Sylhet	1.455**	1.774***	1.350	0.712***	0.679	0.846	0.298**	0.353***	0.276*
	(0.226)	(0.312)	(0.377)	(0.089)	(0.361)	(0.134)	(0.129)	(0.121)	(0.153)
R-squared statistic	n.a.	n.a.	n.a.	n.a.	n.a.	n.a.	0.080	0.068	0.102
Observations	4,877	2,427	2,450	4,877	2,427	2,450	8,887	4,972	3,915

Source: Estimates based on data from the 2006 Bangladesh Urban Health Survey.

Note: Columns (1)–(6) report odds ratios calculated after estimating maximum likelihood binomial logit regressions; columns (7)–(9) report coefficients from estimating ordinary least squares regressions. Regression factors comprise individual, household, and neighborhood-area characteristics, and indicators for administrative divisions. Estimates are adjusted for sampling weights. Robust standard errors, clustered at the neighborhood area level, are reported in parentheses. hdm = household decision-making; CHW = community health worker; hh con = household consumption; n.a. = not applicable; NGO = nongovernmental organization.

a. An individual is classified as "underweight" if the body mass index (BMI) is 17 or lower.

b. An individual is classified as "overweight" if the body mass index (BMI) is 25 or higher.

c. The mental ill-health measure was specially constructed based on the World Health Organization's Self-Reporting Questionnaire (SRQ20). Mental ill-health scores as a continuous variable are used here, logging values to reduce the degree of right skewness in the outcome distribution (zeros were set to 0.1 before the log transformation).

d. The higher decision-making (hdm) authority index variable is constructed by combining data on whether an individual has own or joint decision-making authority over own health services, children's health services, large household purchases, purchases for daily needs, visits to relatives and friends, and food to cook. Separate decision-making authority index variables were constructed for women and men.

e. The housing quality index combines data on flooring, roofing, walls, drinking water source, improved toilet facility, safe garbage disposal, and clean fuel for cooking.

f. The neighborhood-area environmental quality index combines data on the presence of polluting manufacturing units, residential tenure security, sewerage, flooding, water supply, garbage collection, public electrical safety, and public safety in the neighborhood area.

*p < 0.10; **p < 0.05; ***p < 0.01.

Table 3.14 Correlates of Underweight, Overweight, and Mental Ill-Health Status in Men, City Corporations, 2006

Ever-married men, aged 18–49 years

Factor	Underweight[a]			Overweight[b]			Log mental ill-health scores[c]		
	Full (1)	Slum (2)	Nonslum (3)	Full (4)	Slum (5)	Nonslum (6)	Full (7)	Slum (8)	Nonslum (9)
Age	0.976***	0.989	0.946***	1.058***	1.043***	1.072***	0.010**	0.012*	0.006
	(0.008)	(0.008)	(0.015)	(0.011)	(0.015)	(0.016)	(0.005)	(0.006)	(0.006)
Highest ed: preschool–grade 4	0.897	0.890	0.823	1.575	1.124	2.011*	0.072	0.139	-0.122
	(0.123)	(0.125)	(0.282)	(0.448)	(0.416)	(0.770)	(0.078)	(0.087)	(0.146)
Highest ed: grades 5–7	0.898	0.766	1.143	2.050**	1.721*	2.184	0.057	0.048	-0.019
	(0.173)	(0.130)	(0.472)	(0.709)	(0.515)	(1.142)	(0.087)	(0.100)	(0.150)
Highest ed: grades 8–9	0.769	0.663**	0.853	2.351***	2.898***	2.203*	-0.166	0.014	-0.436**
	(0.129)	(0.111)	(0.306)	(0.694)	(0.821)	(1.035)	(0.105)	(0.113)	(0.185)
Highest ed: grades 10–11	0.390***	0.519***	0.296***	2.130***	2.040*	2.175**	-0.524***	-0.320*	-0.800***
	(0.083)	(0.135)	(0.117)	(0.528)	(0.870)	(0.780)	(0.169)	(0.192)	(0.261)
Highest ed: grade 12 or higher	0.214***	0.314**	0.195***	2.189***	2.763***	2.210*	-0.522***	-0.343*	-0.712***
	(0.063)	(0.144)	(0.078)	(0.643)	(0.891)	(0.996)	(0.140)	(0.164)	(0.216)
Moved to current place	0.996	0.975	0.992	0.758	0.881	0.727	-0.041	0.019	-0.067
	(0.144)	(0.135)	(0.304)	(0.157)	(0.262)	(0.219)	(0.072)	(0.085)	(0.108)
Employed	0.717	0.874	0.539	0.853	0.825	1.049	-0.608***	-0.587***	-0.564***
	(0.260)	(0.351)	(0.328)	(0.436)	(0.532)	(0.864)	(0.089)	(0.107)	(0.161)
Own/joint hdm authority score[d]	0.884**	0.882**	0.905	1.198*	1.005	1.314**	-0.031	-0.025	-0.027
	(0.045)	(0.052)	(0.082)	(0.113)	(0.110)	(0.172)	(0.027)	(0.028)	(0.051)
Log mental ill-health score[c]	1.124***	1.133***	1.159**	0.948	0.833**	0.990	—	—	—
	(0.042)	(0.047)	(0.087)	(0.042)	(0.070)	(0.050)			
Household size	0.892***	0.943*	0.810***	1.062	1.030	1.065	0.005	-0.007	0.006
	(0.031)	(0.030)	(0.062)	(0.039)	(0.064)	(0.052)	(0.021)	(0.015)	(0.038)
Housing space per member	0.953**	0.968	0.947	1.023	1.008	1.031*	-0.025***	-0.017*	-0.026***
	(0.019)	(0.019)	(0.037)	(0.015)	(0.034)	(0.018)	(0.005)	(0.009)	(0.006)

table continues next page

Table 3.14 Correlates of Underweight, Overweight, and Mental Ill-Health Status in Men, City Corporations, 2006 *(continued)*

Factor	Underweight[a] Full (1)	Slum (2)	Nonslum (3)	Overweight[b] Full (4)	Slum (5)	Nonslum (6)	Log mental ill-health scores[c] Full (7)	Slum (8)	Nonslum (9)
Housing quality index[e]	0.776***	0.824**	0.696**	1.674***	1.281	1.914***	−0.086*	−0.078	−0.098
	(0.057)	(0.062)	(0.104)	(0.227)	(0.207)	(0.408)	(0.052)	(0.055)	(0.098)
Household faced food shortage	0.994	0.956	0.818	0.611	0.468	1.020	0.376***	0.400***	0.395**
	(0.240)	(0.191)	(0.557)	(0.276)	(0.249)	(0.657)	(0.093)	(0.111)	(0.158)
Log per-member hh con expenditure	0.433***	0.519***	0.280***	1.781**	2.622***	1.470	0.097	0.037	0.160
	(0.055)	(0.084)	(0.057)	(0.506)	(0.590)	(0.528)	(0.067)	(0.060)	(0.103)
Neighborhood-area environmental quality index[f]	0.891*	0.855**	1.043	1.142	1.271*	0.966	−0.038	−0.033	−0.060
	(0.056)	(0.054)	(0.200)	(0.100)	(0.160)	(0.116)	(0.037)	(0.041)	(0.096)
Private pharmacy in neighborhood area	0.898	1.124	0.627	0.642***	0.572**	0.747	0.015	−0.079	0.281
	(0.117)	(0.152)	(0.203)	(0.108)	(0.145)	(0.197)	(0.107)	(0.085)	(0.305)
Private qualified doctor in neighborhood area	0.959	0.753**	1.476**	0.996	0.998	0.996	−0.017	−0.086	0.110
	(0.113)	(0.097)	(0.258)	(0.146)	(0.248)	(0.196)	(0.081)	(0.091)	(0.125)
CHW in neighborhood area	0.853	0.996	0.939	0.896	0.811	0.936	0.124*	0.161*	0.044
	(0.102)	(0.136)	(0.190)	(0.138)	(0.209)	(0.165)	(0.075)	(0.091)	(0.136)
Public health facility in neighborhood area	1.253	1.402	1.178	1.435	2.054***	1.134	−0.041	−0.032	−0.148
	(0.276)	(0.333)	(0.510)	(0.317)	(0.539)	(0.275)	(0.123)	(0.177)	(0.134)
Private health facility in neighborhood area	0.907	1.195	0.523*	1.145	0.910	1.344	0.121	−0.011	0.253*
	(0.139)	(0.163)	(0.190)	(0.222)	(0.281)	(0.344)	(0.088)	(0.095)	(0.133)
NGO health facility in neighborhood area	0.936	0.777*	1.021	1.076	0.993	1.172	0.108	0.078	0.143
	(0.122)	(0.111)	(0.228)	(0.180)	(0.231)	(0.271)	(0.081)	(0.092)	(0.140)
Nonslum neighborhood area	0.986	n.a.	n.a.	1.278	n.a.	n.a.	−0.031	n.a.	n.a.
	(0.121)	n.a.	n.a.	(0.208)	n.a.	n.a.	(0.103)	n.a.	n.a.

table continues next page

Table 3.14 Correlates of Underweight, Overweight, and Mental Ill-Health Status in Men, City Corporations, 2006 (continued)

Factor	Underweight[a]			Overweight[b]			Log mental ill-health scores[c]		
	Full (1)	Slum (2)	Nonslum (3)	Full (4)	Slum (5)	Nonslum (6)	Full (7)	Slum (8)	Nonslum (9)
Barisal	0.769	1.087	0.510	0.639	0.395	0.630	0.153	-0.101	0.582*
	(0.193)	(0.224)	(0.291)	(0.208)	(0.261)	(0.284)	(0.143)	(0.122)	(0.330)
Chittagong	1.314**	1.374**	1.229	1.129	1.189	1.086	0.321***	0.294***	0.359***
	(0.175)	(0.212)	(0.299)	(0.186)	(0.355)	(0.233)	(0.077)	(0.098)	(0.124)
Khulna	1.051	1.230	0.654	1.346	1.486	1.306	0.113	-0.032	0.210
	(0.192)	(0.283)	(0.231)	(0.268)	(0.583)	(0.315)	(0.095)	(0.111)	(0.185)
Rajshahi	0.663*	0.726	0.499	1.387	3.607***	0.833	0.110	0.265*	-0.172
	(0.149)	(0.154)	(0.229)	(0.446)	(1.242)	(0.249)	(0.167)	(0.144)	(0.262)
Sylhet	0.584	1.723*	0.293	0.579**	1.045	0.623*	0.236*	0.317*	0.235
	(0.353)	(0.540)	(0.255)	(0.132)	(0.665)	(0.177)	(0.127)	(0.188)	(0.178)
R-squared statistic	n.a.	n.a.	n.a.	n.a.	n.a.	n.a.	0.082	0.044	0.128
Observations	3,534	1,840	1,694	3,534	1,840	1,694	6,555	3,817	2,738

Source: Estimates based on data from the 2006 Bangladesh Urban Health Survey.

Note: Columns (1)–(6) report average marginal effects calculated after estimating maximum likelihood binomial probit regressions; columns (7)–(9) report coefficients from estimating ordinary least squares regressions. Regression factors comprise individual, household, and neighborhood area characteristics, and indicators for administrative divisions. Estimates are adjusted for sampling weights. Robust standard errors, clustered at the neighborhood-area level, are reported in parentheses. hdm = household decision-making; CHW = community health worker; hh con = household consumption; n.a. = not applicable; NGO = nongovernmental organization.

a. An individual is classified as "underweight" if the body mass index (BMI) is 17 or lower.

b. An individual is classified as "overweight" if the body mass index (BMI) is 25 or higher.

c. The mental ill-health measure was specially constructed based on the World Health Organization's Self-Reporting Questionnaire (SRQ20). Mental ill-health scores as a continuous variable are used here, logging values to reduce the degree of right skewness in the outcome distribution (zeros were set to 0.1 before the log transformation).

d. The higher decision-making (hdm) authority index variable is constructed by combining data on whether an individual has own or joint decision-making authority over own health services, children's health services, large household purchases, purchases for daily needs, visits to relatives and friends, and food to cook. Separate decision-making authority index variables were constructed for women and men.

e. The housing quality index combines data on flooring, roofing, walls, drinking water source, improved toilet facility, safe garbage disposal, and clean fuel for cooking.

f. The neighborhood-area environmental quality index combines data on the presence of polluting manufacturing units, residential tenure security, sewerage, flooding, water supply, garbage collection, public electrical safety, and public safety in the neighborhood area.

*p < 0.10; **p < 0.05; ***p < 0.01.

neighborhood area, having moved to it is associated with a lower likelihood of overweight status for women. Employment is associated with lower mental ill-health scores for men. Employment is also associated with a lower likelihood of overweight status for slum women and with higher mental ill-health scores for nonslum women.

In addition, higher decision-making authority index scores are associated with a lower likelihood of underweight status for slum women and lower mental ill-health scores for nonslum women.[5] They are also associated with a lower likelihood of underweight status for slum men and a higher likelihood of overweight status for nonslum men.

Higher mental ill-health scores are associated with a higher likelihood of underweight status for both men and women. They are also associated with a lower likelihood of overweight status for slum men and nonslum women.

Household Factors

Household size is negatively associated with mental ill-health scores for nonslum women as well as with the likelihood of underweight status for men. Per capita housing space, housing quality index scores,[6] and log per capita household consumption expenditure can all be considered to reflect underlying household economic status. Higher values for these factors tend to be associated with a lower likelihood of underweight status, a higher likelihood of overweight status, and lower mental ill-health scores for both women and men.

Household experience with food shortages in the preceding year is associated with a higher likelihood of underweight status for slum women as well as with higher mental ill-health scores for both women and men. Emerging evidence suggests that stress may be the link between mental ill-health and chronic negative conditions (such as low economic status) or acute negative shocks (such as occurrences of food shortage) (Haushofer and Fehr 2014).

Neighborhood-Area Factors

Whether one resides in a nonslum neighborhood area matters much less frequently when other factors are controlled for, only having a significant negative association with the likelihood of underweight status for women. Neighborhood-area environmental quality index scores do not appear to be associated with outcomes for women.[7] However, they are associated with a lower likelihood of underweight status and a higher likelihood of overweight status for slum men.

Whether the availability of a particular type of neighborhood health service has an influence depends on the specific outcome and sample. The lack of a significant positive association between health service availability and outcomes in many cases may be due to deficiencies in the coverage and quality of preventive health service supply. It may also be due to low household demand for preventive health services. The availability of a particular health service is at times even associated with poorer health outcomes. Such negative associations may indicate the dominant role of reverse causality: that is, neighborhoods with poorer health outcomes attract health services. The negative associations may also be spurious, biased by the regressions' inadequate accounting for other factors that may be correlated with health service availability.

Notes

1. A child is considered to be moderately-to-severely stunted if his or her HAZ is more than two SD below the international reference population median. A child is considered to be severely stunted if his or her HAZ is more than three SD below the international reference population median.

2. The estimated stunting rates are a couple of percentage points off from those reported in the 2013 BUHS, which is suspected to be due to the loss of 100–200 children from the study's sample who were identified to have invalid anthropometric measurements.

3. The 2013 BUHS did not collect information on potentially relevant factors such as (a) for the child, birth weight, diarrhea and treatment, immunization, and deworming; (b) for the mother, physical and mental health (for example, underweight status) and decision-making authority over household expenditures on own and child health as well as over food for the household; and, (c) for the household, food security. The 2006 BUHS collected information on some of these factors; the study finds significant differences in the average levels for several of these factors between slum and nonslum children at that time. Although the effects of access to improved toilets are examined later in the chapter, the BUHS did not gather information on open defecation. Headey and others (2015) find, however, that the area-level open defecation rate is negatively associated with child HAZ, particularly in urban areas of Bangladesh. Although the 2013 BUHS collected information on breastfeeding, the study does not examine the effect of this factor because of limited variation: for children under two years of age, mothers reported that 70 percent were breastfed within an hour of birth, and 94 percent were being breastfed at the time of the survey. Also, because of limited variation in the study data, the study does not include micronutrient supplementation as factors in the regressions: for children under five years of age, 1 percent had received a nutrient mix and 3 percent had received iron supplements in the day before the survey.

4. "Another urban center" is any urban entity other than the current city corporation.

5. As further discussed in chapter 2, index variables were constructed for individual decision-making authority by combining data on whether an individual has own or joint decision-making authority over own health services, children's health services, large household purchases, purchases for daily needs, visits to relatives and friends, and food to cook. Separate decision-making authority index variables were constructed for women and men.

6. As further discussed in chapter 2, the housing quality index combines data on flooring, roofing, walls, drinking water source, improved toilet facility, safe garbage disposal, and clean fuel for cooking.

7. As further discussed in chapter 2, the neighborhood-area environmental quality index combines data on the presence of polluting manufacturing units, residential tenure security, sewerage, flooding, water supply, garbage collection, public electrical safety, and public safety in the neighborhood.

References

Abuya, Benta A., James Ciera, and Elizabeth Kimani-Murage. 2012. "Effect of Mother's Education on Child's Nutritional Status in the Slums of Nairobi." *BMC Pediatrics* 12 (80).

Adams, Alayne M., Herfina Y. Nababan, and S. M. Manzoor Ahmed Hanifi. 2015. "Building Social Networks for Maternal and Newborn Health in Poor Urban Settlements: A Cross Sectional Study in Bangladesh." *PLoS ONE*, 10 (4): e0123817.

Ahsan, Karar Zunaid, Shams El Arifeen, Abdullah Al-Mamun, Shusmita H. Khan, and Nitai Chakraborty. 2017. "Effects of Individual, Household and Community Characteristics on Child Nutritional Status in the Slums of Urban Bangladesh." *Archives of Public Health* 75 (9).

Alam, Mahbub-Ul, Farzana Yeasmin, Farzana Begum, Mahbubur Rahman, Fosiul Alam Nisame, Stephen Luby, Peter Winch, and Leanne Unicomb. 2016. "Can Behaviour Change Approaches Improve the Cleanliness and Functionality of Shared Toilets? A Randomized Control Trial in Dhaka, Bangladesh." Discussion Paper No. 9, Water & Sanitation for the Urban Poor (WSUP), London.

Alam, Narul, Dilruba Begum, Syed Masud Ahmed, and Peter Kim Streatfield. 2011. "MANOSHI Community Health Solutions in Bangladesh: Impact Evaluation Surveys in Dhaka Urban Slums 2007, 2009, 2011." Scientific Report 118, International Center for Diarrhoeal Diseases Research, Dhaka.

Baker, Kelly K., Ciara E. O'Reilly, Myron M. Levine, Karen L. Kotloff, James P. Nataro, Tracy L. Ayers, and others 2016. "Sanitation and Hygiene-Specific Risk Factors for Moderate-to-Severe Diarrhea in Young Children in the Global Enteric Multicenter Study, 2007–2011: Case-Control Study." *PLoS Med* 13 (5): e1002010.

Cattaneo, Matias D., Sebastian Galiani, Paul J. Gertler, Sebastian Martinez, and Rocio Titiunik. 2009. "Housing, Health, and Happiness." *American Economic Journal: Economic Policy* 1 (1): 75–105.

Clasen, Thomas, Wolf-Peter Schmidt, Tamer Rabie, Ian Roberts, and Sandy Cairncross. 2007. "Interventions to Improve Water Quality for Preventing Diarrhoea: Systematic Review and Meta-Analysis." *British Medical Journal* 334 (782).

Dangour, A. D., L. Watson, O. Cumming, S. Boisson, Y. Che, Y. Velleman, S. Cavill, E. Allen, and R. Uauy. 2013. "Interventions to Improve Water Quality and Supply, Sanitation and Hygiene Practices, and Their Effects on the Nutritional Status of Children." *Cochrane Database of Systematic Reviews* 8.

Dewey, Kathryn G., and Daniel R. Mayers. 2011. "Early Child Growth: How Do Nutrition and Infection Interact? *Maternal & Child Nutrition*, 7 (Suppl. 3): 129–42.

Fakir, Adnan M. S., and M. Wasiqur Rahman Khan. 2015. "Determinants of Malnutrition among Urban Slum Children in Bangladesh." *Health Economics Review* 5 (22).

Fewtrell, Lorna, Rachel B. Kaufmann, David Kay, Wayne Enanoria, Laurence Haller, and John M Colford Jr. 2005. "Water, Sanitation, and Hygiene Interventions to Reduce Diarrhoea in Less Developed Countries: A Systematic Review and Meta-Analysis." *Lancet Infectious Diseases* 5: 42–52.

Goudet, Sophie, Paula Griffiths, Barry Bogin, and Nyovani Madise. 2017. "Interventions to Tackle Malnutrition and Its Risk Factors in Children Living in Slums: A Scoping Review." *Annals of Human Biology* 44 (1): 1–10.

Haushofer, Johannes, and Ernst Fehr. 2014. "On the Psychology of Poverty." *Science* 344 (6186): 862–67.

Headey, Derek, John Hoddinott, Disha Ali, Roman Tesfaye, and Mekdim Dereje. 2015. "The Other Asian Enigma: Explaining the Rapid Reduction of Undernutrition in Bangladesh." *World Development* 66: 749–61.

Islam, Mohammad Mainul, and Anita J. Gagnon. 2016. "Use of Reproductive Health Care Services among Urban Migrant Women in Bangladesh." *BMC Women's Health* 16: 15.

Lin, Audrie, Benjamin F. Arnold, Sadia Afreen, Rie Goto, Tarique Mohammad Nurul Huda, Rashidul Haque, and others 2013. "Household Environmental Conditions Are Associated with Enteropathy and Impaired Growth in Rural Bangladesh." *American Journal of Tropical Medicine & Hygiene* 89 (1): 130–37.

Luby, Stephen P., and Amal K. Halder. 2008. "Associations among Handwashing Indicators, Wealth, and Symptoms of Childhood Respiratory Illness in Urban Bangladesh." *Tropical Medicine and International Health* 13 (6): 835–44.

Mishra, Vinod, and Robert D. Retherford. 2007. "Does Biofuel Smoke Contribute to Anemia and Stunting in Early Childhood?" *International Journal of Epidemiology* 36: 117–29.

Mu, Ren, and Alan de Brauw. 2015. "Migration and Young Child Nutrition: Evidence from Rural China." *Journal of Population Economics* 28 (3): 631–57.

NIPORT (National Institute of Population Research and Training), MEASURE Evaluation, ICDDRB (International Center for Diarrheal Disease Research, Bangladesh), and ACPR (Associates for Community and Population Research). 2015. "Bangladesh Urban Health Survey 2013." Final Report, MEASURE Evaluation, Chapel Hill, NC.

Rustein, Shea, and Rebecca Winter. 2014. "The Effects of Fertility Behavior on Child Survival and Child Nutritional Status: Evidence from the Demographic and Health Surveys, 2006 to 2012." DHS Analytical Studies No. 37 prepared for the U.S. Agency for International Development by ICF International, Rockville, MD.

Strunz, Eric C., David G. Addiss, Meredith E. Stocks, Stephanie Ogden, Jurg Utzinger, and Matthew C. Freeman. 2014. "Water, Sanitation, Hygiene, and Soil-Transmitted Helminth Infection: A Systematic Review and Meta-Analysis." *PLoS Med* 11 (3): e1001620.

Zaman, Sultan Uz, Nuhad Raisa Seoty, Masud Alam, Rashidul Haque, and Nawzia Yasmin. 2015. "Household Food Insufficiency and Child Nutritional Status in Urban Slum, Dhaka, Bangladesh." *Acta Medica International*, 2 (1): 65–69.

Ziegelbauer, Kathrin, Benjamin Speich, Daniel Mausezahl, Robert Bos, Jennifer Keiser, and Jurg Utzinger. 2012. "Effect of Sanitation on Soil-Transmitted Helminth Infection: Systematic Review and Meta-Analysis." *PLoS Med* 9 (1): e1001162.

CHAPTER 4

Findings on Urban Health Sector Governance in Bangladesh

Introduction

This chapter presents the findings from an in-depth qualitative assessment of urban health governance in Bangladesh. The analysis aimed to understand how urban health sector governance in Bangladesh is structured and how this affects access, quality, and equity in health service delivery. Annex 4A lists the policy documents, research studies, and other qualitative and quantitative information reviewed for the analysis. The chapter is organized around the three key actors outlined in the health governance framework presented in chapter 2—namely, policy makers, service providers, and citizens.

Policy Makers: Coordination and Stewardship Challenges

The role of the government is central to key health system functions such as regulation, stewardship, and organization. Although the mandate for government engagement in health services is embedded in the Bangladesh's constitution, it is exercised in an ad hoc and fragmented manner in urban settings. The lack of meaningful coordination exacerbates a host of health system quality and equity issues, including its general inability to keep pace with the country's rapid urbanization.

Background

Urban health service in Bangladesh falls under the responsibility of the Ministry of Health and Family Welfare (MOHFW) and the Ministry of Local Government, Rural Development and Co-operatives (MOLGRD&C). MOHFW is the designated ministry for all matters related to health and for ensuring or arranging health services for the entire country, urban and rural. It is responsible for national health-related policy, planning, and decision making on all health issues, which are then implemented by different executing and regulatory authorities. MOHFW also has the stewardship functions of setting technical standards, regulating the sector, and developing policy.

In urban areas, it is responsible for providing policy and technical guidance; setting standards of services; and licensing of private and nongovernmental organization (NGO) health providers (including diagnostic centers, laboratories, and pharmacies) as well as provision of medical supplies, inspections, monitoring, evaluation, and coordination. It is also responsible for the direct provision of urban secondary and tertiary health services.

As for MOLGRD&C, its Local Government Division (LGD) is responsible for providing primary health and public health services specifically in urban areas. The LG/City Corporation Act of 2009 and the Paurashava Act of 2009 clearly mandate that LGD deliver and maintain all social services, including education and basic health services (provision of preventive and promotive health as well as limited curative care and services) in urban areas (ICDDR,B 2015; Kabir, Hossain, and Sabur 2014).[1] However, this vision of its role in urban social service provision is not shared uniformly within MOLGRD&C. Urban governments, as local administrative units governed by elected representatives, have been mandated since the 1960s to provide a wide range of public services to citizens within their jurisdictions and are responsible for the provision and maintenance of basic services and infrastructure in cities and towns.

The Paurashava and City Corporation Acts of 2009 delegate to urban governments many responsibilities that go beyond the basic public health function.[2] In the health sphere alone, these include the maintenance of health systems; the establishment and maintenance of hospitals and dispensaries, health centers, maternity centers, and centers for the welfare of women, infants, and children; provision of training for dais (traditional birth attendants); promotion of family planning; adoption of such other measures as may be necessary to promote the health and welfare of women, infants, and children; and provision of annual registration to private hospitals, clinics, diagnostic centers, and paramedical institutes in their jurisdiction based on the prior approval (No Objection Certificate) from MOHFW's Directorate General of Health Services (DGHS).

Moreover, these mandated responsibilities include waste removal, drain management, road sweeping, control of wild dogs considered dangerous to humans, removal of the carcasses of dead animals, mosquito control, birth and death registration, provision of different certificates, control of food adulteration, sanitation, Expanded Programme on Immunization (EPI) activities, and medical waste management (licensing and renewals to those who collect, transport, and dispose of medical waste).

Perhaps predictably, not all of these provisions of the acts are implemented consistently (table 4.1). LGD provides urban governments with budgetary and management support from the central government, with little participation of urban governments in the planning process. Finally, urban governments receive block grants from LGD for the discharge of their functions, but the grants are not earmarked for health (or any other) services. Nor have clear monitoring and accountability structures been established for the use of these funds.

Table 4.1 Comparison of Provisions and Implementation of Health-Related Mandates in Local Government Acts (Governing City Corporations and Paurashavas) in Bangladesh, 2009

Issue or function	Stated in the act	Implementation of the act
Responsibility for health system	A city corporation or paurashava shall be responsible for the health of the city corporation or paurashava and for this purpose, it may cause such measures to be taken as are required by or under this Ordinance.	Through UPHCSDP, all city corporations (except Chittagong) and selected paurashavas implement this with support from international donors, the central government, and contracted NGOs. There is no separate line for health in city corporation or paurashava budgets.
Hospitals and dispensaries	A city corporation or paurashava may, and if so required by the Government, shall establish and maintain such number of hospitals and dispensaries as may be necessary for the medical relief of the inhabitants of the city corporation or paurashava and the people visiting it.	As there are no rules to implement the act, city corporations and paurashavas do not establish and maintain hospitals and dispensaries.
Registration of private hospitals, clinics, diagnostic centers, and paramedical institutes	With the effectiveness of this Act and hereinafter, any kind of private hospitals, clinics, diagnostic centers, paramedical institute, etc. are not allowed to administer their activities without the registration from the city corporation.	These institutions require approval (No Objection Certificate) from DGH of MOHFW before applying for the registration with the city corporation. Based on the approval, city corporations register them subject to the payment of a specific fee determined by the government.
Registration fees	The city corporation will renew the registration of all private hospitals, clinics, diagnostic centers, paramedical institutes, etc. in condition of submitting the fees determined by the city corporation.	The registration renewal is done yearly with submitting the pre-fixed fees determined by the government. The city corporations impose a penalty of Tk 5,000 if the private institutions fail to register. If the institution does not close the business within the given timeline, Tk 500 per day is charged. The city corporations close them with an arrangement of informing the service recipients; paurashavas are not authorized to undertake such activities like city corporations.
Waste removal, collection, and management	A city corporation or paurashava shall make adequate arrangements for the removal of refuse from all public streets, public latrines, urinals, drains, and all buildings and land vested in the city corporation or paurashava and for the collection and proper disposal of such refuse.	City corporations and paurashavas provide, renew, and in some cases cancel the licenses to the appropriate person or agency for the management and processing of medical waste.

Sources: LG/City Corporation Act of 2009; Paurashava Act of 2009.
Note: DGH = Directorate General of Health Services; MOHFW = Ministry of Health and Family Welfare; NGO = nongovernmental organization; Tk = Bangladesh taka; UPHCSDP = Urban Primary Health Care Services Delivery Project.

Reform Efforts

Although the responsibility for urban health service delivery is shared by MOHFW and MOLGRD&C (the latter through LGD), the lack of meaningful coordination between these ministries significantly constrains the provision of urban health care services, resulting in inadequate health care service coverage for the urban poor. However, the government has taken some promising steps in this regard, mostly related to an enhanced consideration of urban health in policy documents and the creation of coordinating institutional structures:

- *Health, Population and Nutrition Sector Development Program (HPNSDP) 2011–16:* To improve health, population, and nutrition service delivery, in support of the government's third health Sector-Wide Approach (SWAp), the HPNSDP (MOHFW 2011b) included urban health care in its remit, albeit to a limited extent.
- *Urban health focus in National Health Policy 2011 and 7th Five Year Plan (FY2016–FY2020):* Among the priority objectives in recent national health policies and development plans (GED 2015; MOHFW 2011a) is specifically to improve urban health service in order to facilitate access to and the effective use of essential health and family planning services by the urban poor and slum dwellers.
- *National Urban Health Strategy 2014:* To facilitate a shared national vision and common platform for urban health, LGD formulated the National Urban Health Strategy, drafted in 2011 and approved by MOLGRD&C in November 2014 (MOLGRD&C 2014).
- *Urban Health Coordination Committee:* As further discussed below, this interministerial committee was formed in 2015 to strengthen coordination between MOHFW and LGD in facilitating the delivery of essential health services in urban areas.
- *The Fourth Health, Population and Nutrition Sector Program (2017–22):* Recognizing urban health as an emerging challenge, the country's recently approved fourth health SWAp (a) emphasizes the need to expand access to basic health services in urban areas, both through government sources and partnerships with NGOs and the private sector; (b) supports analytical and empirical work on urban health; and (c) includes among its key performance indicators disbursement linked indicators (DLIs) for improved coordination on urban health (GOB 2016; World Bank 2017).

These efforts have so far been limited in their effectiveness. Despite acknowledging the need for effective coordination between MOHFW and MOLGRD&C, the National Urban Health Strategy 2014 does not clearly define the ministries' respective roles, responsibilities, and scope of work. One of its components focuses on "strengthening health service programs of the city corporations and municipalities" and emphasizes the need to "increase the capacity of city corporations and paurashavas so that they can give more attention to public health, preventive health, and family planning services" (MOLGRD&C 2014, 15).

Although the strategy is now being translated into an actionable, time-bound operational plan, MOHFW has not yet endorsed it, and these policy and institutional measures on urban health have certainly not yet translated into effective service delivery.

As for the interministerial Urban Health Coordination Committee (formed under the aegis of MOHFW in 2015, with the secretary of MOHFW as chair and the secretary of LGD as cochair), the committee formed an Urban Health Working Group chaired by the additional secretary of the LGD Urban Development Wing and comprising representatives from city corporations, MOHFW, NGOs, development partners, and the Urban Primary Health Care Services Delivery Project. Nonetheless, challenges persist in following through with the working group's recommendations, including those to strengthen coordination between the two ministries, articulate the operational plans, designate a point person to provide oversight for the urban health sector, and ensure that the working group has the remit and the authority to help achieve these objectives.

Other initiatives are also being explored to strengthen coordination, particularly at the local level, with city mayors taking a leading role in this process. Such an approach is currently being piloted in three municipalities (Jessore, Dinajpur, and Mymensingh) and is showing positive results in terms of the ownership of the initiatives, according to this study's interview data. At the same time, these early experiences highlight the important role that the central government must play in creating a conducive environment for urban governments to be able to effectively manage these initiatives, given their current weak capacity (see also Rahman and Ahmed 2015).

Health-Related Regulation

Urban health system regulation in Bangladesh vis-à-vis both government responsibilities and the rules for the service providers is weak and outdated. Despite the previously mentioned de jure shift of focus toward expanded responsibilities of the urban governments for health systems (rather than purely for sanitation, as originally defined), this has not been supported in reality with a description of their specific responsibilities and parameters. The terminology in the pertinent laws lacks clarity, so it is difficult to say what specifically is delegated—development of the infrastructure, maintenance of facilities, monitoring and accountability, or direct provision of services. More broadly, although urban governments have the mandate for such functions, these are not delegated directly from MOLGRD&C. To overcome this weakness, through the UPHCSDP funded by the Asian Development Bank (ADB), an Urban Health unit was constituted within LGD, although this unit has not been staffed and is therefore not operational.

Regarding the providers, by law, regulation varies widely, depending on whether the health facility is private, NGO-operated, or public. Every private facility that provides health care services and all pharmacies must obtain a license to operate from MOHFW (DGHS or Directorate General of Drug Administration) and a registration with the urban government where the facility is located, which must be renewed every year. However, enforcement is weak, and even when a license is obtained and registration is renewed, this is purely an administrative exercise; no quality controls are conducted in situ to assess the facility's appropriateness and quality. In addition, the Medical Practice, Private Clinics and Laboratories Ordinance that regulates the functioning of private clinics and laboratories prescribes the application process and the criteria for issuing licenses to operate, establishes the maximum applicable fees, dictates inspections, and lists penalties for violations of the rules. However, the ordinance dates back to 1982, and it is not fully enforced (for example, in the case of penalties).

NGO health facilities are regulated under the Voluntary Social Welfare Agencies (registration and control) Ordinance 1961, the Foreign Donations (voluntary activities) Regulation Ordinance 1978, and the Foreign Contribution (Regulation) Ordinance 1982. As such, they must be registered with the NGO Affairs Bureau of the Department of Social Services and need only obtain clearance for health and family planning projects receiving foreign assistance by the Economic Relations Division of the Ministry of Finance and MOHFW.

In contrast, public health facilities have no separate certification process. MOHFW provides an endorsement before establishing the facilities. This is valid for their lifetime. There is no separate licensing process, and, once established, the health service facilities or pharmacies do not require any recertification.

Finally, quality assurance is weak, and monitoring and evaluation is fragmented. The provisions for quality control, such as licensing and accreditation, are noted in existing regulations but are not effectively enforced. The monitoring and evaluation function is not coordinated at the central level.

It would be difficult to measure the whole urban health system's performance, at any rate, because so much essential data are either unavailable or inadequate. The national Health Management Information System (HMIS), residing within MOHFW, covers all MOHFW facilities in rural and urban areas but does not capture data from the other government health facilities or from NGO or private facilities. The information collected by NGO providers is mainly reported to donor-funded project administrators rather than to MOHFW, making it extremely difficult to measure those providers' performance within the urban health system or to use their data for decision making. This issue is recognized as a major challenge, and discussions have started on possible ways to address it. For example, some pilot locations within the Urban Health Systems Strengthening Project (UHSSP), led by Options Consultancy Services UK, are starting to work toward having a common reporting mechanism by using an adapted District Health Information Software, version 2 (DHIS2), so that data from all service providers in certain areas are captured and reported uniformly, and municipalitywide dashboards can be created to monitor aggregate performance (UHSSP 2015). Joint visits to the facilities are conducted to check data quality.

Health Service Providers and Financing: Fragmented Service Delivery

The delivery of urban health services is also characterized by fragmentation and the coexistence of a great variety of service providers, especially at the primary health level. The urban primary health system is made up of parallel programs and structures of MOHFW, LGD (of MOLGRD&C), and several national and international NGOs. MOHFW provides services through secondary and tertiary hospitals in all divisional cities and at district and subdistrict health facilities. Its role in primary health care services is, however, limited to community clinics at the union level (Adams, Islam, and Ahmed 2015);[3] 35 government outdoor dispensaries (limited mostly to Dhaka and Chittagong city corporations); and some outpatient services in secondary and tertiary public hospitals.

As noted earlier, urban governments have legal and administrative mandates to carry out public responsibilities, including primary health services (ADB n.d.). Each city corporation and paurashava has a Health Department, headed by a chief health officer (CHO) and assisted by medical officers, several paramedics, and other staff to deal with public and environmental health, basic sanitation, and water supply. However, the Health Department often has insufficient resources and authority, and no proper job description and clear lines of authority, to effectively provide public health services.

Private providers (both formal and informal), including a broad range of facilities from private for-profit providers to NGOs, deliver an important share of primary health services to the urban population. Pharmacies are often the first point of contact of the population with the health system. Critical ongoing urban health initiatives implemented by NGOs include the UPHCSDP; the Smiling Sun Franchise Program (SSFP), supported by the U.S. Agency for International Development (USAID) and U.K. Department for International Development (DFID) through the NGO Health Service Delivery Project (NHSDP); NGO facility- and community- based programs in the slums by Building Resources Across Communities (BRAC), particularly the BRAC Manoshi program; and the Marie Stopes Clinics for sexual and reproductive health services.

Among these NGO health service programs in Bangladesh, BRAC, for example, uses female community health workers (CHWs) to provide maternal and child services to the urban slum population in Dhaka, but the quality of services and the engagement of the CHWs has been variable (Alam, Tasneem, and Oliveras 2012). An additional service delivery challenge relates to the ability of such programs to retain health care workers, which is influenced by a mix of financial incentives, social prestige, community approval and positive feedback from patients, and household responsibilities (Alam and Oliveras 2014).

Availability, Quality, and Equity of Care

The availability of health facilities for the country's urban population varies between metropolitan cities and district towns, in terms of size and type of facilities. The metropolitan or divisional headquarters offer all categories of services—from primary care to tertiary-level hospitals, including specialized hospitals. Primary and secondary health service is available in the smaller cities. In addition to modern allopathic medicine–based services, traditional or alternative medicine practitioners like homeopathic and Ayurvedic or Unani practitioners also offer limited health services.[4]

In Dhaka city, the most dominant provider is the UPHCSDP, implemented through NGO clinics. In Chittagong, the other metropolitan city (discussed further in box 4.1), NGOs have a smaller presence than in Dhaka. In the relatively smaller district towns, primary health services through NGOs are minimal. The poor rely on government facilities for primary health services. For normal child delivery at a nominal cost, the poor and the middle class depend on NGOs and local government facilities.

Box 4.1 Primary Health Care Services for the Urban Population: The Chittagong Model

Chittagong is the second largest city, and one of the major coastal ports, in Bangladesh. With a population of approximately 5 million, Chittagong city corporation (hereafter Chittagong) is rapidly becoming urbanized. It is divided into 41 wards, covering 185 square kilometers. Chittagong has approximately 210 slum settlements where over 1 million people live.

Extent of Primary Health Services

Chittagong provides primary health services to its urban population through 1,100 health staff working in 5 maternity hospitals, 1 general hospital, 56 primary health centers and dispensaries, and 336 EPI centers. There is at least one primary health center in each of the 41 wards, providing outpatient services. From fiscal year (FY) 2010 through FY2014, the 20 charitable dispensaries provided primary health services to a total of 280,503 patients, averaging 10 outpatient visits per charitable dispensary per day. In addition, Chittagong runs 9 homeopathic charitable dispensaries and 1 charitable homeopathic hospital. During 2010–14, 145,312 patients (10 patients per facility per day) sought health services from these facilities. At least 60 percent of the homeopathic services are free and targeted to the poor, with a focus on women and girls.

A Tradition of Dynamic Leadership

Dhaka and Chittagong municipalities were established in 1864 and 1863, respectively. Discussions with local government experts revealed that Chittagong has differed from Dhaka since even before the 1947 partition. Because Dhaka was designated as the capital city, many of its urban services became a part of the central government system, while Chittagong municipality had to provide its own services to the population. Therefore, one of Chittagong's unique features was its leadership.

Historically, several mayors have provided dynamic leadership in expanding health service coverage as well as diversifying the revenue sources for these services. In 1928, the local

box continues next page

Box 4.1 Primary Health Care Services for the Urban Population: The Chittagong Model *(continued)*

government activity chart had prioritized health and education, which later became institutionalized as city programs. In 1994, Mohiuddin Chowdhury, who became Chittagong's first democratically elected mayor, successfully extended and implemented health and education programs, mainly with funding generated from taxation and from entrance and utilization fees for public places; characteristic of Chittagong is its focus on using its own assets to generate income. During this period, additional specialized health facilities and training centers were established, including the first health care technology training center in Bangladesh. Chittagong was also the first city in which a private university was established.

Launch of Urban Health Project

In 1998, the government of Bangladesh introduced the UPHCSDP. This ADB-funded initiative involves public-private partnerships with national NGOs to improve the health status of the poor in city corporations and selected municipalities by providing an essential package of services.

Chittagong participated in the first two stages of the project (1998–2005 and 2005–11). However, during the third phase (2012), Chittagong opted out once its request to implement the project directly through its preexisting health infrastructure was rejected by LGD and the ADB. Hence, Chittagong decided to be a direct provider of services, making it a unique case in the Bangladesh urban health landscape.

Financing of City Health Expenditures

Chittagong generates revenues from its own resources, development grants, and other sources including donations (respectively 55.5 percent, 38.4 percent, and 6 percent in FY 2015/16); municipal tax and other taxes constituted 68 percent of its revenue from own sources (37.8 percent of the total income) in FY 2015/16. Its own income is generated from treatment plants, shopping malls, compressed natural gas or petrol stations, housing projects, and children's parks, among others.

Its health-related entities also generated revenue, which accounted for 1.4 percent of the revenue from own sources (0.8 percent of total income). In FY2015/16, 1.1 percent of Chittagong's total expenditure was on health-related activities and entities (excluding spraying for mosquito control). However, health-related expenditure as a proportion of health-related income is 0.7 percent.

Reporting

Chittagong's health service data, apart from EPI data and certain primary health data, are not sent to MOHFW because the city no longer participates in UPHCSDP. Chittagong has an internal reporting system, which is reviewed monthly. A monthly report is sent to MOLGRD&C only.

Replicability and Sustainability of the Chittagong Model

Chittagong has consistently prioritized and developed its health infrastructure. It may be difficult to replicate this model in other parts of urban Bangladesh because of the lack of preexisting public infrastructure, unless the government is willing to make a large investment in

box continues next page

Box 4.1 Primary Health Care Services for the Urban Population: The Chittagong Model *(continued)*

developing health infrastructure. However, the financial sustainability of the model in the long run needs to be explored.

Chittagong will likely struggle to run the network of primary health facilities because of budgetary pressures due to maintenance costs associated with satellite clinics at the community level that may gradually fall into disuse. The user fees in Chittagong's hospitals, which now provide free or subsidized care, may also increase. It is unclear whether, in the long run, this model will be financially sustainable without an intervention from the central level.

On the other hand, the NGO-contracting model operating in the rest of the country's urban areas does not seem to be sustainable, either. Without government investments in sustainable health infrastructure, NGOs themselves do not have the necessary incentives to develop those facilities. In addition, NGOs are typically focusing on the delivery of a subset of health services, mainly related to maternal and child health, while urban areas have an increasing need to broaden the spectrum of services offered in a more integrated way.

Sources: Chittagong City Corporation Annual Report 2015; the official website of the Chittagong City Corporation: http://www .ccc.org.bd/; and study informant interviews.

Unsurprisingly, given this widespread fragmentation of providers and services, the health care service delivery system in urban areas is uncoordinated and does not provide comprehensive care. In terms of horizontal integration, there is no sign of facilities working together to provide a comprehensive range of services to the population in their areas. In terms of vertical integration, the referral system is rudimentary, and patients often opt to access specialized care directly without referrals, as our study interviews revealed.

> The referral system does not exist. Sometimes the patients are referred to higher-level facilities, but they do not receive any preferred treatment and the facility does not refer them back. Therefore, those who can afford to go to the higher-level facilities, go there directly.

> —Study informant: independent expert, Bangladesh health system

As for health service offerings, all facilities in urban areas are required by MOHFW to provide an essential service package. However, there are gaps in the types of services offered by the facilities: because service provision has generally focused on maternal and child health services, other groups are left underserved (including male adults) and other health concerns and conditions overlooked (such as prevention, risk factors, and noncommunicable disease). While this is an important gap on the supply side, it has also negatively affected the demand for health services overall because it has reinforced the perception that primary health facilities are not the appropriate place for groups other than mothers and children to seek care.

We mainly get female patients. Men don't want to come to clinics because there is a perception that the facility and its services are more oriented to women and children. Men prefer going to pharmacies.

—Study informant: representative of NHSDP partner NGO, Chittagong

The quality of care is variable, and the quality assurance mechanisms that do exist are not enforced effectively, the qualitative analysis found. Regulations on licensing and accreditation exist, but licenses are mostly provided by a desk review of the documents, and rarely supported by rigorous quality control checks. Monitoring of service quality and performance reporting is difficult because it is unclear how many facilities in urban areas report to the national health information system. Within facilities, there are no standardized systems for quality assurance, and patients have no clear and reliable mechanisms for providing feedback on the quality of services. Nor do the professional associations seem to play the strong role that they might to ensure compliance with quality of care norms and adherence to standards of practice as well as to promote relevant behavior change among health service professionals.

Given that many providers are under contract to donor-driven projects, reporting is mainly through parallel vertical systems. The national government lacks a complete picture of the health services provided and the related outputs and outcomes. Consequently, there is no mechanism for feeding data and advice back to the lower-level facilities for the required course corrections.

To reduce the fragmentation of the system, MOHFW could work with MOLGRD&C to map all formal urban health facilities, which in turn could enable assignment of responsibility for the health service needs of the population in the designated catchment area of a given facility (empanelment). Although this may be difficult to implement, especially given the mobility of many urban residents, it could still provide a basis for establishing a functioning public sector referral system. It could also help in establishing capitation payments for public facilities, albeit not for NGOs and private facilities, which generate their own revenues. The provision of primary health care services through Chittagong Municipal Corporation is a notable exception, which could perhaps offer lessons, although the replicability of this model is questionable (box 4.1).

Health System Financing

Regarding financing, the city corporations and paurashavas do not have a separate line item for health in their budgets; health-related activities are embedded in functions such as waste removal, mosquito control, and so on. Within these line items, the budget for health is limited to purchasing medicines and chemicals for supplying in emergencies, for use as disinfectants, for pathology tests, and for health-related national day observances.

Among their more prominent functions, the health departments of city corporations deliver vaccinations under the World Health Organization's (WHO) EPI through their health assistants and paramedics. The vaccines are provided by the DGHS, and the city corporations distribute the vaccines to various EPI centers and bear the transportation costs.

An urban government has sanctioned posts for paramedics and one doctor,[5] and salaries come from its own revenue sources and from donor-funded projects implemented by NGOs. This practice is in line with the overall administrative organization in the country, which does not have fiscal decentralization, and there is no local participation in the resource allocation function. Streamlining the financing for the urban health sector would seem to be a necessary precondition for a fully functioning system.

Community: Gaps in Citizens' Health-Seeking Behavior, User Satisfaction, and Voice

Health-Seeking Behavior

For an illness at its early stage, particularly if it is not too painful physically, most patients in Bangladesh—especially the poor—forgo visits to a physician. For minor illnesses, patients usually seek care from the private sector. Pharmacies are de facto the first line of contact for minor illnesses, and the preferred choice, especially for men. Only when an ailment persists, or becomes serious, do patients decide to visit a qualified physician.

The selection of an allopathic practitioner running a private practice as the health service provider is often based on the knowledge and perception of family and friends. The presence of an acquaintance as a staff member in a health facility can also be a determining factor. The type of illness also plays a key role in the selection of a private provider. For serious illnesses, which normally require inpatient care, government facilities are most often the preferred choice, because of the availability of qualified physicians and the lower out-of-pocket costs, especially for the poor.

The nonpoor prefer private health facilities, as they are willing to pay a higher price for shorter waiting periods, a cleaner environment, and competent doctors. The poor and the less-educated urban residents are inclined to wait longer before visiting a qualified doctor. They tend to be less cognizant of the dangers of delaying medical intervention and are distressed about the high cost of visiting private facilities—which may well turn them down if they cannot pay the fees. One of our informants recalled this type of experience.

> My child was refused access to a doctor in a private clinic as I did not have the full fee for the doctor (Tk 500). I could offer no more than Tk 400.
>
> —Female interviewee, Mohakhali, Dhaka

Distance from the health facility and the cost of services are two important factors in household selection of health service providers. Overall, availability of facilities near the place of residence does not seem to be an issue in most urban areas. However, to secure the services of a preferred physician, patients compromise on the inconvenience to themselves and their attendants of traveling to a more-distant facility. Referrals, when given, are viewed as advisory and not a statutory obligation. Under the Bangladesh health system's citizen charters (to be discussed further), citizens are entitled to seek treatment from any public hospital, so many patients from smaller towns and rural areas opt to go to Dhaka, even if it entails a longer travel distance, with the expectation of better treatment.

User Satisfaction

The level of patients' satisfaction varies by facility and provider, determined by perception and experience relating to cost, distance, waiting period, behavior of health personnel, hygiene, and health outcomes following the visit (table 4.2).

Both the poor and the nonpoor are aware that the physicians employed in public hospitals are well-qualified, and many of the senior doctors are nationally renowned. Most of the study's informants considered the availability or access to doctors in those facilities to be limited and uncertain; however, they were confident that any technical input from these medical personnel in terms of diagnosis, treatment, and prescription of drugs would be effective, especially when care was sought before, but unsuccessfully, from informal providers or pharmacists.

Table 4.2 Patient Perceptions of Health Facility Strengths and Weaknesses in Urban Bangladesh, by Type

Facility type	Strengths	Weaknesses
Public facilities	• Low cost • Qualified doctors	• Shortage of doctors • Insufficient time given by doctors to patients • Doctors behave poorly with poor patients • Long waiting time • Exploitation by middlemen • Unhygienic conditions (of floors, rooms, equipment) • Medicine often must be purchased from outside hospital • Diagnostic tests frequently must be done outside hospitals as equipment needs repair • Limited beds for inpatients
Private facilities	• Qualified doctors • More-flexible timing • Doctors are well behaved • Cleaner than public facilities	• Unqualified pharmacy personnel • Higher costs • Forced to do many costly laboratory tests • Some not equipped to deal with complicated health issues • Do not want to deal with patients involved in accidents
NGO facilities	• Easy access and low cost • Doctors are well behaved • Cleaner than government facilities	• Limited services with strong focus on RMNCH services

Sources: Study informant interviews.
Note: NGO = nongovernmental organization; RMNCH = reproductive, maternal, newborn, and child health.

I bought a drug from a pharmacy, but it did not cure me; the same medicine was given to me at the government hospital, and it worked.

—Female interviewee, Satpai, Netrokona Sadar

On the other hand, overcrowding and the paucity of space were viewed as major constraints of public hospitals. The limited bed capacity means that patients must wait for long periods (ranging from several hours to even days) before a bed is allotted. Most of the interviewees from poor as well as nonpoor households expressed concerns about the unhygienic conditions at government hospitals. The hospital cleaners cannot keep up with keeping the wards, corridors, and restrooms clean and hygienic, partially because of the overcrowding. The frequent unavailability of medicines in the public hospital is another area of uniform dissatisfaction.

Nevertheless, those who received inpatient health services from public facilities expressed satisfaction with the admissions process. Especially when patients are referred by another hospital, getting admitted to a public hospital did not seem to be a problem. The exception, however, involved those admitted as emergency patients due to accidents, because of the bureaucracy associated with the record keeping of accidents and the number of forms that must be completed for the police before such patients can be admitted.

The long waiting periods to receive outpatient primary health services is a major bone of contention. It is more distressing for those who travel long distances and lack the family support to attend to their household chores or therefore must forgo work. Outpatient service recipients complain about the inadequate time allocated by the medical personnel during their visits. The shortage or absence of female doctors discourages many from visiting Mother and Child Welfare Centre (MCWC) facilities—entities under the Directorate of Family Planning of MOHFW that offer outpatient and limited inpatient services for mother and child. Some of the poor women interviewed conveyed their negative experience during child delivery at government facilities.

One of the study's interviewees recalled how she was rushed to a Medical College Hospital in Dhaka for an emergency C-section. She had to travel a long distance, using public transportation. Her unclean attire and sweaty body irked the nurses and the physician. They rebuked her during the entire C-section procedure. When recounting her stressful experience, she stated, "I'd rather die than go to a government hospital in the future. Poor people have nobody but Allah to rely upon."

Misbehavior by doctors or facility staff is a major grievance of the poor who seek care in a public hospital. When people were asked to comment on the quality of care they received, they responded positively if the doctor had given time to listening to their problems, provided free medicine, or if the outcome of the treatment matched their expectations. Those who participated in the group interviews viewed the behavior of the support staff in public hospitals poorly. They alleged that many of these personnel ask for tips and bribes, without which service would not be provided.

The infrastructural inadequacies in the number and quality of public facilities create an adversarial environment that encourages rent-seeking behavior within as well as outside the facility. Hospital staff can become arrogant and less caring, using the alibi that they are attending to more demands than existing resources would enable; ultimately, they are not held accountable for the quality of care provided. External actors such as middlemen ("dalals") and politically, socially, or administratively influential people use their acumen or contacts to access the services for their clients. Corruption also permeates the system; thus, many of the public health facilities are poorly governed, and the weakest voices are those of the poor and the disadvantaged.

> Accountability is not in the mindset of the providers. Government officials, including those working in the health sector, have a specific mental scheme: they are accountable to their superior, but not to the citizen. The government intention, though, is that every facility have some sort of a committee [with participation of different community representatives], but they are not functioning. So, for urban health, the mayor and the elected commissioners, who are involved in developing the system, are accountable to their constituencies and will make these committees accountable. If enough demand can be created [from the bottom-up], this can also trigger the commitment.
>
> —Study informant: UHSSP officer, Dhaka

Patients seem to be mostly content with the quality of treatment provided by private practitioners. Many interviewees believe that the number of diagnostic tests suggested by private physicians are necessary, although it is alleged that many doctors receive a commission or a share of the revenue from laboratory tests. The high cost of visits, and the physicians' insistence on laboratory testing in a private facility, is viewed as a financial burden. Often the urban nonpoor seek primary care services from private practitioners at their chambers. Patients prefer them for being accessible and for giving them an opportunity to discuss their issues in detail and develop a personal rapport.

Most of the NGO hospitals are viewed favorably for their affordability, overall cleanliness, good behavior of health attendants, and the skilled professionals. The limited number of services offered by NGOs is the main complaint and source of frustration for patients. The urban poor and the middle-class individuals interviewed would like to see an increase in the number of NGO health facilities offering a wider range of preventive and curative care services. In general, the poor are satisfied with NGO facilities because of easy access and affordability. The poor also perceive the quality of NGO health services to be good, and they do not feel disrespected by virtue of their social status. Some of the lower-middle-income families, as well as the poor, expressed satisfaction with hospitals established through public-private partnerships or as a charitable trust.

NGOs offer outpatient services at prescribed hours that are often inconvenient, because they are incompatible with work. Irrespective of economic status, patients appreciate the good behavior of doctors and other staff at private and NGO inpatient facilities, who are viewed as more attentive to the needs of the patient than the staff at public facilities. Private and NGO hospitals are usually perceived as cleaner and more secure than government hospitals. However, NGO and most for-profit hospitals (except tertiary care hospitals like Apollo and United) are viewed to have relatively less-skilled staff than those at public hospitals.

Voice

The socially and economically well-placed are treated better at public facilities, because they are willing and able to pay tips and bribes or to use their personal connections and political influence. The poor, however, are in a much weaker position. Their lower social and economic status makes them vulnerable to unfriendly behavior from hospital personnel and subject to long waiting periods for the same services that wealthier patients receive quickly. Health providers do not feel threatened by potential reprisals from dissatisfied poor patients. The poor and the less educated are least aware of the citizen charter (discussed subsequently) and of their rights and responsibilities in relation to health providers.

Discussions with the poor suggest that they are bereft of a collective voice in expressing their grievances and complaints. They are either not aware of existing mechanisms to file complaints or have no confidence in their effectiveness. On the contrary, filing a complaint is viewed as a risky proposition, as patients may be deprived of the service in the process. Local community leaders, including elected officials, are not willing to confront health service providers to file a complaint. In addition, given the frequency of migration of poor households within or outside a city, it is difficult to create and maintain a sense of ownership in a community that may be changing frequently.

In cases of extreme negligence leading to serious complications or death at a health facility, the community may get aggrieved and the local leaders may become involved. However, the influential person is likely to become vocal only if the patient is personally known. Such a collective complaint is almost always a transitory affair, with little bearing on fundamental reforms that would ensure greater accountability of providers and better health service for the poor.

> Doctors to fourth grade staff are all generally politically connected. Hence, it is not possible to take administrative measures against them.
>
> —Study informant: civil surgeon in a district town

Hospital Management Committees exist in each district to monitor the performance of government secondary and tertiary health facilities. Each committee is headed by a member of parliament and comprises representatives of different stakeholders, including junior and senior medical personnel, elected local officials, and NGO representatives. The committee is expected to meet each month and address issues ranging from infrastructure, hygiene, and waste management to quality of services, including the review of grievances submitted in the complaint box. However, there is a lack of commitment or interest among the committee members, and meetings are not held regularly, primarily because of the unavailability of the member of parliament. This mechanism has generally proved to be ineffective in delivering on its objectives.

The major departments of public hospitals have a citizen charter. The charter provides specific guidelines or instructions on services to be provided. These have been implemented with some success, but not all commitments listed in the charters are honored by the hospitals. For example, under the citizen charter for Medical College Hospitals Emergency Department (MCH-ED), the MCH-ED must be open 24 hours a day and provide treatment to the patient before doing any administrative work (table 4.3). However, because of the shortage of beds and medical staff, this is not always maintained. Patients also reported they were often asked to complete admission forms, including providing information required by the police, before receiving care.

Table 4.3 Provisions and Observations of Citizen Charter for Medical College Hospitals Emergency Department

Citizen charter	Field observations or findings
1. Emergency department will be open 24 hours a day, and patients will be provided treatment immediately.	Yes, this service is offered.
2. After the patient has been provided immediate treatment, other administrative work can be done.	Yes, this service is offered.
3. Sufficient number of full-time medical officers should be there.	Yes, this service is offered.
4. All patients who need to be admitted are admitted.	Yes, this service is offered. However, there is a shortage of beds. Hence patients occupy hospital floors to receive treatment.
5. Nurses, paramedics, ward boys, and other support and maintenance staffs are available at the casualty department for emergency patients.	Yes, this service is offered. However, there is a shortage of staff due to (a) understaffing or (b) lack of regulation in monitoring staff's activities.
6. If a patient dies while on the way to the hospital, he will be declared "brought dead" and legal proceedings will take place in an appropriate manner.	Yes, this service is offered. However, the implementation of the proceedings often results in difficult and complicated situations for the attendant.
7. Patients of road accidents, failed suicides, and any other cases which are called police cases will be provided with treatment.	Yes, this service is offered. However, the implementation of this provision and reporting often results in difficult and complicated situations for the attendant. The treatment is delayed due to incomplete adherence to the reporting requirements.
8. If an unidentified patient or unconscious patient passes away after being brought in and there is no attendant with him, his belongings will be entrusted to the medical officer.	Yes, this service is offered.
9. In different wards/departments there will be a hung list of stock of drugs, principal services, and doctors.	Yes, it is offered. However, patients are not aware of the list and services.

Sources: Citizen charter of Medical College Hospitals Emergency Department (MCH-ED); MCH-ED field visit observations.

The charter also ensures that "nurses, paramedics, ward boys, and other support and maintenance staffs are available at the casualty department for emergency patients." However, many of the hospitals are still understaffed, and ward boys and other support and maintenance staff are not always available, because of the poor implementation of the regulation. Most patients are unaware of the available stocks of drugs, the principal services they are entitled to, and the list of doctors on duty—information that is supposed to be displayed in different wards and departments (table 4.3).

> To improve services in government hospitals, the number of specialist doctors needs to be increased, and their availability has to be ensured. Legal measures to reduce the nuisance of agents and middlemen are a must.
>
> —Focus group participant, NGO representative

NGOs appear to be more accountable to citizens' concerns than public health facilities. Several factors contribute to a relatively friendly environment. Most NGOs are dependent on donor funding or funding through the government (for example, for family planning commodities). Any controversy or complaints can adversely affect their relationship with their financiers. Senior management at NGOs accordingly monitor citizens' complaints. Marie Stopes and Ahsania Mission representatives observed that they publicly display telephone numbers that patients can call to file complaints. Follow-up action is usually taken by the management against grievances. The USAID-supported Shurjer Hashi clinics have citizens' committees, represented by community leaders. These committees meet with clinic officials periodically, and their members individually or collectively address concerns or make suggestions for improvements. However, NGOs clearly avoid treating patients suffering from acute pain or serious ailments, referring such patients to nearby public hospitals. Through their established network, BRAC clinics help poor patients to get admitted to tertiary hospitals.

Throughout Bangladesh's urban health system, even though citizen groups formally exist, they do not seem to serve the interests of all groups. Cultural norms play an important role in defining which groups can express their views and whose voices can be heard. However, in more informal settings a different picture emerges, which does not always find a way to reach the formal channels of feedback and therefore remains unheard.

Citizens do not seem to trust the system, but turn instead to their personal networks for advice on where to seek care. They often delay care and, when seeking care because of repeated or persistent problems, they normally access informal providers and pharmacists first—a finding that is in line with other studies (for example, Ahmed and others 2010). Finally, they perceive the referral as a mere suggestion, do not see any additional benefits to following the referral, and eventually bypass the system.

Financial barriers to access persist, and are not being addressed in a coherent fashion. For example, exemptions from user fees exist; but, on the one hand, it is very difficult to identify the poor who can benefit from those and, on the other, exemptions are not applied consistently across facilities.

Although citizen charters are present, not all provisions are enforced, and there are no reliable mechanisms to hold facilities accountable. Citizens are usually unaware of their rights. In addition, culturally, it is not considered legitimate behavior to question the quality of care that is received, especially if it is provided by a doctor. The way people usually react to poor quality of care received is by visiting a different provider the next time they need care rather than by providing feedback in the first place.

Conclusion

This chapter presented how governance structures in urban Bangladesh are influencing the way health services (particularly at the primary care level) are organized and delivered and how citizens are empowered—or not, in this case—to hold the urban health system accountable for its services and results. The study has highlighted challenges pertaining to all three groups of key actors in our health governance framework:

- *Government policy makers:* Consistent with other studies, we find a lack of effective mechanisms for coordination between the MOHFW and the MOLGRD&C, specifically through the LGD, and a rather modest stewardship role taken by the MOHFW so far.
- *Service providers:* The range of services offered are fragmented and limited, exhibiting an inadequate ability to plan and respond to the needs of some patient and population groups. The quality of services is highly variable, and it's impossible to assess the overall performance of the system because of parallel or partial reporting structures.
- *Citizens:* A culture of accountability is yet to be developed. Some mechanisms for feedback and citizens' voice do exist de jure, but de facto are either not used, not trusted by the population, or do not represent the interest of all groups.

The following chapters will reflect further on the overarching findings from the quantitative analysis of the social determinants of health and nutrition and from the qualitative "deep dive" into urban health governance, and offer potential recommendations for policy options.

Annex 4A Bibliography for Qualitative Analysis of Urban Health Governance

Abt Associates. 2012. "Health Systems 20/20: Final Project Report." Report prepared by Abt Associates Inc., Bethesda, MD, for the Health Systems 20/20 Project, U.S. Agency for International Development, Washington, DC.

Adams, Alayne M., Rubana Islam, and Tanvir Ahmed. 2015. "Who Serves the Urban Poor? A Geospatial and Descriptive Analysis of Health Services in Slum Settlements in Dhaka, Bangladesh." *Health Policy and Planning* 30 (Suppl 1): i32–i45.

ADB (Asian Development Bank). 2015. "Proposed Results-Based Loan and Administration of Technical Assistance Grant. India: Supporting National Urban Health Mission."

Report and Recommendation of the President to the Board of Directors (Project No. RRP IND 47354-003), ADB, Manila.

———. n.d. "Local Government Institutional Assessment." Project document, Urban Primary Health Care Services Delivery Project (No. RRP BAN 42177), ADB, Manila. https://www.adb.org/sites/default/files/linked-documents/42177-013-ban -oth-03.pdf.

Agarwal, Siddharth. 2011. "The State of Urban Health in India: Comparing the Poorest Quartile to the Rest of the Urban Population in Selected States and Cities." *Environment & Urbanization* 23 (1): 13–28.

Ahmed, Syed Masud, Bushra Binte Alam, Iqbal Anwar, Tahmina Begum, Rumana Huque, Jahangir A. M. Khan, Herfina Nababan, and Ferdaus Arfina Osman. 2015. *Bangladesh Health System Review.* Health Systems in Transition Series Vol. 5, No. 3. Geneva: World Health Organization.

Ahmed, Syed Masud, Awlad Hossain, Marufa Aziz Khan, Malay Kanti Mridha, Ashraful Alam, Nuzhat Choudhury, Tamanna Sharmin, Kaosar Afsana, and Abbas Bhuiya. 2010. "Using Formative Research to Develop MNCH Programme in Urban Slums in Bangladesh: Experiences from MANOSHI, BRAC." *BMC Public Health* 10: 663.

Ahmed, Syed Masud, Kuhel Faizul Islam, and Abbas Bhuiya, eds. 2014. *Urban Health Scenario: Looking Beyond 2015.* Bangladesh Health Watch Report 2014. Dhaka: Bangladesh Health Watch Secretariat, James P. Grant School of Public Health, BRAC University.

Ahsan, Karar Zunaid, Peter Kim Streatfield, Rashida-E-Ijdi, Gabriela Maria Escudero, Abdul Waheed Khan, and M. M. Reza. 2016. "Fifteen Years of Sector-Wide Approach (SWAp) in Bangladesh Health Sector: An Assessment of Progress." *Health Policy and Planning* 31 (5): 612–23.

Alam, Khurshid, and Elizabeth Oliveras. 2014. "Retention of Female Volunteer Community Health Workers in Dhaka Urban Slums: A Prospective Cohort Study." *Human Resources for Health* 12: 29.

Alam, Khurshid, Sakiba Tasneem, and Elizabeth Oliveras. 2012. "Performance of Female Volunteer Community Health Workers in Dhaka Urban Slums." *Social Science and Medicine* 75 (3): 511–15.

Bangladesh Health Watch. 2016. *Non-Communicable Diseases in Bangladesh: Current Scenario and Future Directions.* Bangladesh Health Watch Report 2016. Dhaka: Bangladesh Health Watch Secretariat, James P. Grant School of Public Health, BRAC University.

Cairncross, Sandy, and Vivian Valdmanis. 2006. "Water Supply, Sanitation, and Hygiene Promotion." In *Disease Control Priorities in Developing Countries*, second edition, edited by D. T. Jamison, J. G. Breman, A. R. Measham, G. Alleyne, M. Claeson, D. B. Evans, P. Jha, A. Mills, and P. Musgrove, 771–92. Washington, DC: World Bank and Oxford University Press.

Chowdhury, Mahbub Elahi. 2016. "Contribution of the MOHFW for Urban Health Services: Gaps and Possible Solutions." Policy Brief, International Centre for Diarrhoeal Disease Research, Bangladesh (ICDDR,B), Dhaka.

Dalpatadu, Shanti, Prasadini Perera, Ruwani Wickramasinghe, and Ravindra P. Rannan-Eliya. 2015. "Public Hospital Governance in Sri Lanka: A Case Study on Processes and Performance." In *Public Hospital Governance in Asia and the Pacific*, edited by D. Huntington and K. Hort. 257–99. Comparative Case Studies Vol. 1, No. 1. Geneva: World Health Organization.

DGHS (Directorate General of Health Services). 2015. "Health Bulletin 2015." Annual publication, Management Information System, DGHS, Ministry of Health and Family Welfare, Government of Bangladesh, Dhaka.

GOB (Government of Bangladesh). 2012. *Bangladesh Population & Housing Census 2011—National Census Report, Volume-4: Socio-Economic and Demographic Report.* Dhaka: Bangladesh Bureau of Statistics, GOB.

ICDDR,B (International Centre for Diarrhoeal Disease Research, Bangladesh). 2015. "Technical Assistance for Assessment of Contribution of Ministry of Health and Family Welfare for Urban Health Services." Final report, ICDDR,B, Dhaka.

————. "Urban Health Atlas." (Accessed October 10, 2017), http://urbanhealthatlas .com/.

IIPS (International Institute for Population Sciences) and Macro International. 2007. "National Family Health Survey (NFHS-3), 2005–06: India. Volume I." NFHS-3 national report, IIPS, Mumbai.

Islam, Mursaleena, Mark Montgomery, and Shivani Taneja. 2006. "Urban Health and Care-Seeking Behavior: A Case Study of Slums in India and the Philippines." Final Report prepared by Abt Associates Inc., Bethesda, MD, for the Partners for Health Reformplus Project, U.S. Agency for International Development, Washington, DC.

Islam, Nazrul. 2012. "Urbanization and Urban Governance in Bangladesh." Background paper for 13th Annual Global Development Conference on "Urbanization and Development: Delving Deeper into the Nexus." Budapest, June 16–18.

Kabir, Humayun, A. K. Mohammad Hossain, and Muhammod Abdus Sabir. 2014. "Strengthening Stewardship Functions of the Regulatory Bodies under MOHFW." Final study draft prepared for the Ministry of Health and Family Welfare (MOHFW), Government of Bangladesh, Dhaka.

Kenyan Healthcare Federation. 2016. "Kenyan Healthcare Sector. Market Study Report: Opportunities for the Dutch Life Sciences & Health Sector." Study commissioned by the Embassy of the Kingdom of the Netherlands in Nairobi (Publication No. RVO-138-1601/RP-INT), Netherlands Enterprise Agency, Ministry of Foreign Affairs, The Hague.

Mberu, Blessing U., Tilahun N. Haregu, Catherine Kyobutungi, and Alex C. Ezeh. 2016. "Health and Health-Related Indicators in Slum, Rural, and Urban Communities: A Comparative Analysis." *Global Health Action* 9: 33163.

Micheal, Jonga. 2013. "When Environmental Sanitation Threatens Water Safety: Lessons from Korail Slum Dhaka City." *Water and Sanitation* (blog), November 28. https:// jonmii.wordpress.com/2013/11/28/when-environmental-sanitation-threatens -water-satety-lessons-from-korail-slum-dhaka-city/.

MOHFW (Ministry of Health and Family Welfare). 2005. "National Drug Policy 2005." Notification of No. Public Health-1/Drug-22/2004/154, published in *Bangladesh Gazette*, 440–53.

————. 2015. "Bangladesh National Health Accounts 1997–2012." BNHA-IV report, Research Paper No. 42a, Health Economics Unit, MOHFW, Government Bangladesh, Dhaka.

MOLGRD&C (Ministry of Local Government, Rural Development and Co-operatives). 2012. "Development Project Proposal (DPP), Urban Primary Health Care Services Delivery Project (UPHCSDP)." Part B. MOLGRD&C, Government of Bangladesh, Dhaka.

————. 2014. "National Urban Health Strategy 2014." Strategy document, MOLGRD&C, Government of Bangladesh, Dhaka. http://uphcp.gov.bd/cmsfiles/files/NUHS.pdf.

Montekio, Victor B., Guadalupe Medina, and Rosana Aquino. 2011. "The Health System of Brazil." [In Spanish.] *Salud Publica de Mexico* 53 (Supp. 2): s120–s131.

Mullen, Patrick, Divya Nair, Jayati Nigam, and Katyayni Seth. 2016. "Urban Health Advantages and Penalties in India: Overview and Case Studies." Discussion Paper No. AUS7433. World Bank, Washington, DC.

NIPORT (National Institute of Population Research and Training), MEASURE Evaluation, International Centre for Diarrhoeal Disease Research, Bangladesh (ICDDR,B), and ACPR (Associates for Community and Population Research). 2015. "Bangladesh Urban Health Survey 2013." Final report, MEASURE Evaluation, Chapel Hill, NC.

NIPORT (National Institute of Population Research and Training), Mitra and Associates, and ICF International. 2016. "Bangladesh Demographic and Health Survey 2014." Dhaka, Bangladesh; Rockville, MD: NIPORT, Mitra and Associates, and ICF International.

PAHO/WHO (Pan American Health Organization/World Health Organization). 2008. "Health Systems and Services Profile, Brazil: Monitoring and Analysis of Health Systems Change/Reform." Country health systems profile, PAHO/WHO, Brasilia.

Paim, Jairnilson, Claudia Travassos, Celia Almeida, Ligia Bahia, and James Macinko. 2011. "The Brazilian Health System: History, Advances, and Challenges." *Lancet* 377 (9779): 1778–97.

Rahman, Hossain Zillur, and Tofail Ahmed. 2015. "Strategy on Local Government Strengthening: Background Paper for 7th Five Year Plan." Background paper, Power and Participation Research Center, Dhaka.

Roy, T., L. Marcil, R. H. Chowdhury, K. Afsana, and H. Perry. 2014. "The BRAC Manoshi Approach to Initiating a Maternal, Neonatal and Child Health Project in Urban Slums with Social Mapping, Census Taking, and Community Engagement." Guidebook, Building Resources Across Communities (BRAC), Dhaka.

Terra de Souza, Ana Cristina, E. Cufino, K. E. Peterson, J. Gardner, M. I. Vasconcelos do Amaral, and A. Ascherio. 1999. "Variations in Infant Mortality Rates among Municipalities in the State of Ceara, Northeast Brazil: An Ecological Analysis." *International Journal of Epidemiology* 28 (2): 267–75.

UHSSP (Urban Health Systems Strengthening Project). 2015. "Institutional Capacity Development Assessment: Urban Local Government Institutes and Associated Actors in Three Cities of Bangladesh (Baseline)," UHSSP, Dhaka.

UN DESA (United Nations Department of Economic and Social Affairs). 2004. *World Urbanization Prospects: The 2003 Revision.* New York: United Nations.

Vaughan, Patrick J., Enamul Karim, and Kent Buse. 2000. "Health Services Systems in Transition III. Bangladesh, Part I. An Overview of the Health Care System in Bangladesh." *Journal of Public Health Medicine* 22 (1): 5–9.

WHO (World Health Organization). 2000. *The Management of Nutrition in Major Emergencies.* Geneva: WHO.

————. 2008. *Closing the Gap in a Generation: Health Equity through Action on the Social Determinants of Health.* Final Report of the Commission on Social Determinants of Health. Geneva: WHO.

World Bank. 2007. "Bangladesh. Dhaka: Improving Living Conditions for the Urban Poor." Report 35824-BD, World Bank, Washington, DC.

———. Bangladesh Country Data, World Bank Open Database (accessed October 10, 2017), https://data.worldbank.org/country/bangladesh.

———. India Country Data, World Bank Open Database (accessed October 10, 2017), https://data.worldbank.org/country/india.

———. Urban Population Data (from United Nations *World Urbanization Prospects*), World Bank Open Database (accessed October 10, 2017), https://data.worldbank .org/indicator/SP.URB.TOTL.IN.ZS.

Notes

1. The urban local government institutions are the paurashava (municipality) for district and subdistrict (upazilla) level and city corporation at the divisional city and, in some cases, for larger districts. At present, there are 11 city corporations and 320 paurashavas in Bangladesh.

2. The functions of urban governments broadly relate to *public health* (such as water supply and sewerage and sanitation); *public welfare* (such as public facilities for education and recreation); *regulation* (enforcing building bylaws, encroachments on public land, and so on); *public safety* (fire protection, street lighting, and the like); *public works* (construction and maintenance of roads, culverts and drainage systems, and so on); and *development activities* (such as town planning and development of commercial markets).

3. The union is the smallest rural administrative and local government unit in Bangladesh. Each union is made up of nine wards. Usually one village is designated as a ward. There are 4,554 unions in Bangladesh.

4. Throughout this report, the discussion is limited to modern allopathic medicine–based service providers.

5. The number of paramedics depends on the size of the center as well as the volume of work for running the health services.

References

Adams, Alayne M., Rubana Islam, and Tanvir Ahmed. 2015. "Who Serves the Urban Poor? A Geospatial and Descriptive Analysis of Health Services in Slum Settlements in Dhaka, Bangladesh." *Health Policy and Planning* 30 (Suppl 1): i32–i45.

ADB (Asian Development Bank). n.d. "Local Government Institutional Assessment." Project document, Urban Primary Health Care Services Delivery Project (No. RRP BAN 42177), ADB, Manila.

Ahmed, Syed Masud, Awlad Hossain, Marufa Aziz Khan, Malay Kanti Mridha, Ashraful Alam, Nuzhat Choudhury, Tamanna Sharmin, Kaosar Afsana, and Abbas Bhuiya. 2010. "Using Formative Research to Develop MNCH Programme in Urban Slums in Bangladesh: Experiences from *MANOSHI*, BRAC." *BMC Public Health* 10: 663.

Alam, Khurshid, and Elizabeth Oliveras. 2014. "Retention of Female Volunteer Community Health Workers in Dhaka Urban Slums: A Prospective Cohort Study." *Human Resources for Health* 12: 29.

Alam, Khurshid, Sakiba Tasneem, and Elizabeth Oliveras. 2012. "Performance of Female Volunteer Community Health Workers in Dhaka Urban Slums." *Social Science and Medicine* 75 (3): 511–15.

Chittagong City Corporation Annual Report. 2015. Chittagong, Bangladesh. http://www .ccc.org.bd/.

GED (General Economics Division). 2015. "7th Five Year Plan, FY2016–FY2020: Accelerating Growth, Empowering Citizens." Planning document, GED, Planning Commission, Government of Bangladesh, Dhaka.

GOB (Government of Bangladesh). 2016. "Health, Nutrition and Population Strategic Investment Plan (HNPSIP), 2016–21." Planning Wing, Ministry of Health and Family Welfare, Government of Bangladesh, Dhaka.

ICDDR,B (International Center for Diarrheal Disease Research, Bangladesh). 2015. "Technical Assistance for Assessment of Contribution of Ministry of Health and Family Welfare for Urban Health Services." Final report, ICDDR,B, Dhaka.

Kabir, Humayun, A. K. Mohammad Hossain, and Muhammod Abdus Sabur. 2014. "Strengthening Stewardship Functions of the Regulatory Bodies under MOHFW." Final study draft prepared for the Ministry of Health and Family Welfare (MOHFW), Government of Bangladesh, Dhaka.

MOHFW (Ministry of Health and Family Welfare). 2011a. "National Health Strategy 2011." [In Bengali.] Strategy document, MOHFW, Government of Bangladesh, Dhaka.

———. 2011b. "Strategic Plan for Health, Population & Nutrition Sector Development Program (HPNSDP), 2011–2016." Strategy document, Planning Wing, MOHFW, Government of Bangladesh, Dhaka.

MOLGRD&C (Ministry of Local Government, Rural Development and Co-operatives). 2014. "National Urban Health Strategy 2014." Strategy document, MOLGRD&C, Government of Bangladesh, Dhaka.

Rahman, Hossain Zillur, and Tofail Ahmed. 2015. "Strategy on Local Government Strengthening: Background Paper for 7th Five Year Plan." Paper by the Power and Participation Research Centre, Dhaka.

UHSSP (Urban Health Systems Strengthening Project). 2015. "Institutional Capacity Development Assessment: Urban Local Government Institutes and Associated Actors in Three Cities of Bangladesh (Baseline)." UHSSP, Dhaka, Bangladesh.

World Bank. 2017. "Bangladesh Health Sector Support Project." Project appraisal document No. PAD2355, World Bank, Washington, DC.

CHAPTER 5

Summary of Findings

Health and Nutrition Outcomes and Determinants

The collective evidence indicates that average child nutrition status (measured by under-five child height-for-age z-scores, or HAZ) and socioeconomic conditions are substantially poorer for slum residents than nonslum residents. Average levels of child HAZ, mother's education attainment, household wealth, access to and availability of health-protective household amenities, use of maternal and child health services, and neighborhood-area environmental quality are all lower for slum residents than nonslum residents.

Child age, mother's age at childbirth, mother's education attainment, and household wealth have significant effects on child HAZ. The nonslum neighborhood-area advantage in child HAZ remains significant even after accounting for a range of child, mother, household, and neighborhood-area factors. Facility-based antenatal care has a significant positive effect on child HAZ. However, the size and significance of this effect varies by health facility (that is, by public, nongovernmental organization [NGO], or private health facility) and by whether the neighborhood area is slum or nonslum. Irrespective of health facility type and area, facility-based delivery and newborn exam have insignificant effects on child HAZ. Access to improved toilets that is shared with many other households has a significant negative effect on slum child HAZ, whereas a handwashing site at the dwelling with soap and water has a significant positive effect on nonslum child HAZ.

Among the adult health outcomes, the study finds that certain factors stand out in terms of significant effects (positive or negative) on more than one outcome or for more than one sample. At the individual level, such factors include age, high education attainment, and mental ill-health. At the household level, they include household economic status and household experience with food shortages. At the neighborhood-area level, they include neighborhood-area environmental quality and health service availability.

The slum versus nonslum distinction of the neighborhood area matters for fewer outcomes and samples than when unconditional slum-nonslum differences in average outcomes are examined. Administrative divisions matter despite the inclusion of an extensive set of factors in the regressions.

A shortcoming of the analysis is that the regressions predict a small fraction of the variation in health and nutrition outcomes. R-squared statistics from estimating regressions based on ordinary least squares for all outcomes and samples indicate that less than 20 percent of the variation in outcomes is predicted by the included factors. In addition, the predictive power of the regressions is much worse for slum residents than nonslum residents. These results indicate the need to identify additional potential factors, especially for slum residents. Although the study was able to examine a large set of factors in the regressions, the factors are mostly conventional in nature. More extensive data on behavioral risk factors, health-promoting and health-damaging behaviors (including health care–seeking behaviors), and health- and health care–related beliefs at the individual, parental, and household head levels may help to strengthen the predictive power of the regressions.

Stewardship and Governance

Two important challenges pertaining to the stewardship and planning function are (a) a paucity of meaningful coordination between the Ministry of Health and Family Welfare (MOHFW) and the Ministry of Local Government, Rural Development and Co-operatives (MOLGRD&C) on the provision of urban health services; and (b) the inability of the urban health system—particularly at the primary health level—to keep pace with urbanization. These factors contribute to the inadequate numbers and poor quality of public facilities, which, along with the high cost of private health facilities, frequently result in the denial of basic health services to the urban poor.

Some promising steps have been taken in this regard, mostly related to greater consideration of urban health in policy documents as well as the creation of coordinating institution structures. For instance, as noted in chapter 2, one of the priority objectives of the National Health Policy 2011 as well as the "7th Five Year Plan, FY2016–FY2020" is specifically to improve urban health services (GED 2015; MOHFW 2011). Further, to facilitate a shared national vision and common platform for urban health, the Local Government Division (LGD) of MOLGRD&C formulated the National Urban Health Strategy 2014 (MOLGRD&C 2014). However, this strategy has yet to be endorsed by the other national ministry overseeing health services: MOHFW.

Despite the creation of an interministerial Urban Health Coordination Committee and an Urban Health Working Group to strengthen coordination between MOHFW and LGD and facilitate the delivery of essential health services in urban areas, challenges persist in terms of following through with the recommendations from these bodies. Hopefully, the Fourth Health, Population and Nutrition Sector Program (2017–22)—with a disbursement linked indicator (DLI) focused on urban coordination—will provide the needed impetus. Other initiatives are also being explored to strengthen coordination, particularly at the local level, with city mayors taking a leading role in this process. These experiences highlight the critical role that the central government must play in creating a conducive environment for urban governments to be able to effectively manage these initiatives, given their current weak capacity.

In terms of financing, urban governments do not have a separate line item for health in their budgets. Each urban government has sanctioned posts for paramedics and one doctor,[1] and salaries come from their own sources of revenue and from donor-funded projects implemented by NGOs. This is in line with the overall administrative organization in the country, which does not have fiscal decentralization, and there is no local participation in the fund allocation function.

The following steps could be considered to streamline the financing for the urban health sector, as a necessary precondition for a fully functioning health system:

- Standardizing the methods used to identify the poor and the level of exemption from user fees and to ensure compliance of providers
- Updating and standardizing user fees for essential services and the most common procedures
- Aligning financing better with responsibilities for urban health, as most funding currently comes from international donors, not directly from MOLGRD&C
- Establishing proper financing from the central budget that targets the delivery and coordination of planned health services—given that urban governments play a more active role in planning for health services—and exploring options to complement those funds with revenues collected at the local level (for example, in Chittagong) while being mindful of the centralized processes in place in Bangladesh

Finally, overall regulation of the urban health system appears weak and outdated. Despite the de jure shift of focus toward urban governments' expanded responsibilities for health systems (rather than purely for sanitation), this has not been supported by a description of their specific responsibilities and parameters. And although private health care providers and pharmacies are required to obtain a license to operate from MOHFW (Directorate General of Health Services and Directorate General of Drug Administration, respectively) and to annually renew a registration with the urban government where the facilities are located, enforcement is weak, and no quality controls are conducted in situ. Public facilities, on the other hand, have no separate certification process, with a mere one-off endorsement provided by MOHFW before the establishment of the facilities.

Service Delivery Organization

Bangladesh has spent much energy on defining which government agencies should play an active role in urban health service provision. However, service delivery is just one of several fundamental health system functions; others such as stewardship, regulation, financing, and quality assurance also require appropriate government intervention and oversight, predominantly through MOHFW. Furthermore, the delivery of urban health services by public facilities in Bangladesh (as in many other low- and middle-income countries) is often insufficient to satisfy the demand and need for such services.

Given the insufficient number and quality of the public facilities, especially those delivering primary health services, many private providers have entered the field. There is a strong need to regulate these providers, to understand how they are performing, and to ensure convergence toward higher quality across the range of providers.

The structure of the health delivery system is suboptimal. It is characterized by the presence of different legal entities with low levels of horizontal and vertical integration and a nonexistent referral system; the lack of focus on continuity of care, patient-centeredness, and integrated approaches; and the unavailability of services for certain conditions and patient groups (including men and patients with noncommunicable diseases), given the strong focus of the delivery system on reproductive, maternal, and child health services. The reliance of NGOs on donor funding is a limiting factor that prevents their facilities from offering a broader range of services to a wider population.

The NGO contracting-out model, common in nearly all urban areas in Bangladesh, presents some important challenges. These are more apparent with the Urban Primary Health Services Delivery Project model financed by the Asian Development Bank, but they are generally applicable to the other urban health models in Bangladesh as well. These challenges include the following:

- *Sustainability*—not just financial sustainability but also related to the rapid turnover of staff, poor design and management as well as short duration of contracts, an inadequate focus on incentives and quality of care, and day-to-day financial management pressures on NGOs
- *A fragmented reporting system*, which constrains analytics and effective decision making
- *Difficulty in assessing the real coverage of urban health services*, since services are also provided to rural patients, with overlapping service providers in the same catchment area (for example, in Khulna)
- *Unsuitable facility opening hours* for most working urban residents
- *Limited range of service offerings*, since most primary health facilities are focused on reproductive, maternal, newborn, and child health (RMNCH) services
- *Difficulties in systematically identifying the poor* in communities served to ensure exemptions from out-of-pocket payments
- *Poorly standardized user-fee exemptions*, which are usually contractually mandatory and applied to 30 percent of users

Unsurprisingly given its fragmentation, the health service delivery system in urban areas is uncoordinated and does not provide comprehensive care. There is no shortage of facilities at the primary health level (although there is clearly scope for increasing the *availability* of facilities, especially in the newer districts [MOHFW 2014]). However, facilities do not have a clear catchment population, and therefore the system gives people no guidance on where to go first for care; rather, they are left on their own to decide where to seek care. Nor is there any planning at the local government level to avoid duplication of services between facilities serving the same communities or to ensure that these facilities offer a comprehensive range of services to the population in their areas. In terms of vertical integration, the referral system is dysfunctional. Patients have access to specialized care even without the referral and, even when they do have the referral, it appears that they often disregard it or, in any case, do not follow it.

Quality of care varies by provider and by facility, and quality assurance mechanisms are not enforced effectively. Some regulation requiring licensing and accreditation exists, but it is not enforced uniformly and should be updated. The monitoring and evaluation function is not coordinated at the central level. Within the facilities, there are no clear and consistent mechanisms for quality assurance, reporting, and dealing with complaints. This is consistent with findings from other recent assessments of the sector (such as MOHFW 2014). Professional associations could play a bigger role in promoting a stronger patient-centered culture among providers, but this is yet to happen on a large scale.

Given that many providers are contracted by donor projects, reporting is still mainly through vertical programs. The central government does not have a complete picture of the services provided and the related outputs and outcomes. Therefore, there is no mechanism for feeding data back to the lower levels and to facilities for course corrections.

To reduce the fragmentation of the system, MOHFW recently expressed the intention of working with MOLGRD&C to map all formal urban health facilities to assign the responsibility to care for the population in the catchment area to a given facility (empanelment). Although this will be difficult to implement, especially considering the mobile nature of many urban residents, it could provide a basis for establishing a functioning referral system with the use of capitation payment for the public facilities. NGO and private facilities will continue to generate their own revenues, as they are currently doing.

Responsiveness and Accountability

The fragmentation of the service delivery system poses an additional challenge: it cannot provide care in an integrated manner. There has been an increasing global focus on the promotion of patient-centered and integrated models of care, which ensure continuity and coordination, as an essential step toward the progressive realization of universal health coverage. As Bangladesh moves toward universal health coverage, there is a recognition among policy makers and researchers alike that such elements are fundamentally compromised in urban Bangladesh: Patients do not enter the system from a designated point and are not guided through it. The coordination among facilities is weak, given the difficulties in enforcing empanelment of mobile populations and the nonexistence of a referral and counter-referral system.

There has been inadequate emphasis on the accountability of the system—and no clarity on patients' rights. Care is provided episodically with no focus on prevention and the patients' responsibility for their health and well-being. No sense of trust is established between the provider and the patients over the course of time, and the relationship is hierarchical. Patients delay seeking care and turn to their personal networks for advice first; when reaching out to the health system, their first points of contacts are often private pharmacies. Patients lack a clear and reliable way of providing feedback on quality of services, and in some cases fear retaliation if they do provide feedback. As such, patients usually react to the poor quality of care received by visiting a different provider the next time they need care rather than by providing feedback in the first place.

Patient groups exist formally, and are helpful to some extent; however, often they do not ensure that all perspectives are voiced adequately. Often, while representatives from all patient groups might be part of those groups, sociocultural norms dictate who can speak and whose voices are therefore heard. Perhaps there should be different mechanisms to ensure the representation and voice of separate groups.

Overall, the culture of accountability is weak. To start shifting this mentality, it will be important to work not only on the supply side (changing the mind-set of the providers and of the government) but also on the demand side by increasing citizens' awareness of their rights and responsibilities.

The next chapter examines the policy implications of these findings and explores policy options that the government of Bangladesh might consider to improve urban health care.

Note

1. Number of paramedics depend on the size of the center and on the volume of work for running the health services.

References

GED (General Economics Division). 2015. "7th Five Year Plan, FY2016–FY2020: Accelerating Growth, Empowering Citizens." Planning document, GED, Planning Commission, Government of Bangladesh, Dhaka.

MOHFW (Ministry of Health and Family Welfare). 2011. "National Health Policy 2011." [In Bengali.] MOHFW, Government of Bangladesh, Dhaka.

———. 2014. "Draft National Health Policy 2015." [In Bengali.] MOHFW, Government of Bangladesh, Dhaka.

MOLGRD&C (Ministry of Local Government, Rural Development and Co-operatives). 2014. "National Urban Health Strategy 2014." Strategy document, MOLGRD&C, Government of Bangladesh, Dhaka.

CHAPTER 6

Looking to the Future

Policy Implications and Options

Overall, urbanization and the urban health milieu in Bangladesh have evolved rapidly, without a concurrent emerging vision of how the urban health system should work. As such, there is a pressing need to develop a shared urban health policy in consultation with relevant stakeholders.

In addition to underlining a stronger stewardship role for the government, the study findings suggest that existing urban health policies need to better reflect the evolving operating environment, including increasingly relevant issues such as rural-urban migration; the changing epidemiological and demographic profiles of urban areas; the expansion and proliferation of slum settlements; the potential for multisectoral action to influence health and nutrition indicators; the unique urban governance structures; the needs of a working population; and the health human resource, financing, and service provision realities on the ground.

Importance of Nutrition-Sensitive Interventions

Fairly consistent international evidence exists on the large positive effect of mothers' education on child nutrition status. For example, using microdata for a large set of low- and middle-income countries (LMICs), Alderman and Headey (2017) find that the effect of mothers' education on child nutrition status increases with years of education, is larger than the effect of fathers' education, and is larger in countries with high stunting rates.

Maternal education is theorized to affect child nutrition status through a household income effect arising from higher labor earnings, which the study attempts to control for based on household asset–based wealth. Maternal education is also theorized to affect child nutrition status through the direct delivery of health and nutrition information; delayed age of marriage and age at child's birth; greater ability to acquire, absorb, and apply health and nutrition information from other sources; greater openness to reproductive, maternal, newborn, and child health (RMNCH) services; greater decision-making authority within the household with respect to food, health, and care; and access to more-educated social networks (Ruel, Alderman, and the Maternal and Child Nutrition Study Group 2013). Using data from a slum settlement in Dhaka, Fakir and Khan (2015) find that the effect of a mother's education attainment on child underweight status appears to be partially mediated through her knowledge of health-promoting behaviors. Our data do not allow us to test potential pathways. Nevertheless, the results suggest that policies and programs that aim to raise girls' education attainment are appropriate and should receive greater priority.

Similarly, fairly consistent international evidence exists on the large positive effect of household economic status on child nutrition status. Cash transfers is one way to raise household income. The international evidence of the effects of unconditional and conditional cash transfer programs in LMICs is mixed, and the overall effect on child height is small and insignificant (Manley, Gitter, and Slavchevska 2013). However, the review also finds that the overall effect of transfer programs is larger (albeit not always statistically significant) for the youngest children and girls; for children in households with longer program participation; and in settings with poorer health outcomes and health service use at baseline, when transfers are conditioned on health service use. These insights on the variation of effects are useful for program design. In addition, Alderman and Headey (2017) find that mothers' education and household wealth are generally complements in LMICs, suggesting that policies and programs that succeed in raising household income may also raise the child nutrition payoffs from parental education attainments.

The evidence suggests that the development and improvement of nutrition-sensitive programs is key. The nutrition sensitivity of programs can be enhanced by incorporating explicit nutrition goals and by targeting women and children who are more nutritionally vulnerable from a physiological perspective (Ruel, Alderman, and the Maternal and Child Nutrition Study Group 2013). Given that slum residents face multiple disadvantages in their conditions, saturating slum settlements with a wide array of nutrition-sensitive programs may be needed to generate large, durable nutrition gains. Such an ambitious goal notwithstanding, nutrition-specific interventions should remain an integral part of the policy package for slum residents. In their review of the international evidence, Goudet and others (2017) find that nutrition-specific interventions in slum settlements—such as micronutrient supplementation, nutrition promotion, school feeding, and treatment of acute malnutrition—tend to have positive effects on child nutrition status.

Among the various other nutrition-sensitive areas, water, sanitation, and hygiene (WASH) amenities, services, and practices stand out as critical for improving the health and nutrition status of urban residents, in particular slum residents. Poor urban WASH services are a major threat to public health. Although open defecation is negligible in urban Bangladesh, toilet facilities are often shared among households in common. The new dimensions of the urban sanitation problem lie in keeping shared toilets clean and usable and providing wide, safe, and reliable formal fecal sludge management (FSM) services across the entire chain, from proper containment in on-site toilet facilities and emptying to treatment and disposal (Peal and others 2014).

Relatively easy and inexpensive interventions such as door-to-door behavior-change communication campaigns, combined with basic provisions at toilet facilities such as flush and water storage buckets and signage, have been shown to dramatically improve the cleanliness of shared toilets in slum settlements in Dhaka (Alam and others 2016). Such interventions and others based on careful, context-specific formative research would need to be developed to address the many and often complex sources of environmental risks to health that house-holds face. Formal, well-functioning FSM services will first and foremost require government regulatory actions, coupled with models to strengthen private FSM services, and interventions to stimulate household demand for FSM services (Ross, Scott, and Joseph 2016).

Role of Government Stewardship
In addition to developing and updating health system policies, the government at all levels struggles with timely implementation and enforcement of policies and regulations. Therefore, it is important that existing and future policies be enforced more consistently, accompanied by the establishment of viable clinical quality assurance mechanisms as well as periodic Ministry of Health and Family Welfare (MOHFW) audits to monitor provider compliance with standards, in collaboration with the relevant professional associations.

Given the critical roles of MOHFW, Ministry of Local Government, Rural Development and Co-operatives (MOLGRD&C), and urban governments in urban health, especially at the primary health level, it is fundamental to delineate clearly their respective responsibilities and improve their coordination at both the national and local levels, perhaps building on existing or new models. The aim should be to understand and implement at scale practical ways of ensuring coordination and ownership at the local levels, with the active participation of local governments, while recognizing the differences among cities of different sizes. Such action would strengthen accountability of the system by delegating more responsibilities to local governments, which are closer to communities. The coordination efforts should include international donors that have been sup-porting specific urban health projects in Bangladesh. At the same time, MOHFW has an important role to play in providing technical leadership and support to this process, while helping to build capacity at the local level.

Other vital, albeit often overlooked, priorities include the need to raise citizen awareness about their rights and responsibilities for their own health and well-being (for example, the right to receive care with dignity, the risks of delaying medical care, the importance of prevention, and the availability of various services and facilities available as well as costs and fee exemptions). In addition, it is impor-tant to ensure the participation of beneficiaries in the design and implementation of effective urban health service delivery systems. Citizen engagement is pivotal for setting up a system that can respond to their evolving needs. Although Bangladesh has quite a centralized system, the example of Brazil could be helpful, insofar as decentralization in the country (which has been relatively successful) was in fact demanded first and foremost by civil society (World Bank 2003).

To better support government decision making, data systems, quality, and reporting also need to be strengthened, leveraging existing technology to the extent possible. Routine monitoring should be combined with operations research and periodic survey-based evaluations. Bangladesh has already established a national Health Management Information System, which collects data from rural areas and from secondary and tertiary health facilities in urban areas. It would be important to consolidate information on urban *primary* health services through this system so that information can flow to the central level and be fed back to the lower levels and to facilities. Meanwhile, there are some promising initiatives on collecting additional data more consistently from the various urban primary health facilities through the rollout in 2014 of the Bangladesh Demographic and Health Survey (DHS) 2014 (NIPORT, Mitra and Associates, and ICF International 2016); it would be worthwhile to consider the possibility of building on such experiences.

Lessons from Health Service Providers

In rural Bangladesh, nongovernmental organizations (NGOs) have accumulated decades of experience in health development, achieving success from continuous learning and adaptation of interventions. In urban Bangladesh, where NGOs are more recently engaged in primary health services, they face a similar learning process—one that can be instructive to all providers of urban health service delivery.

Notwithstanding, the health development record in rural Bangladesh is mixed. Although the government and NGOs have been especially successful in promoting family planning through contraceptives, infectious disease prevention through vaccinations, and diarrheal treatment through oral rehydration, they have been less successful in other areas of maternal and child health and in addressing maternal and child undernutrition (El Arifeen and others 2013). Hence, there is an even greater need for iterative learning from testing interventions for improving the quality and increasing the use of health services—whether the provider is public, NGO, or private—by the urban poor and slum residents. The scope of such interventions needs to move beyond maternal and child health services to also respond to the epidemic of noncommunicable diseases as well as reach out to underserved groups, including men.

Most households in urban Bangladesh, including poor ones, seek health care from private providers. Therefore, policies, programs, and partnerships should aim particularly to ensure quality of care among such providers. A variety of (typically small-scale) interventions have been tested in different LMIC settings with the aim of improving the utilization and quality of private health services. These interventions include social marketing, vouchers, franchising, regulation, accreditation, and contracting.

Although empirical evidence remains scarce on the effects of these interventions—and the evidence that exists is generally of poor quality (Madhavan and others 2010; Patouillard and others 2007)—recent rigorous evidence is promising. For example, Bennett and Yin (2014) and Björkman-Nyqvist, Svensson, and Yanagizawa-Drott (2012) find that the entry of better providers motivates incumbent private providers to respond by improving quality and reducing prices in local drug markets. Under an experimental evaluation, Das and others (2016) find that general training offered to informal private health providers in rural West Bengal, India, increased correct case management for selected common conditions (respiratory distress, child diarrhea, and chest pain) based on information gathered from standardized patients.

Based on the above discussion, the government of Bangladesh could consider several strategic directions relevant to the various facets of urban health. Table 6.1 summarizes these directions.

Getting There from Here: Charting a Way Forward

Based on the findings of this study and the strategic options identified, a four-pronged approach is presented here for charting an initial way forward on urban health in Bangladesh and helping the country realize its universal health coverage aspirations. While these recommendations are not intended to be prescriptive, the study's findings suggest that an exploration of these options could be a useful starting point for a more comprehensive and inclusive dialogue on urban health policy.

Establishing an Institutional Structure for Delivery of Urban Health Services
Putting Urban Governments at the Center of Primary Health Service Delivery

Urban governments in Bangladesh have been mandated to provide social services, including primary health services, in urban areas. Urban governments also have the advantage of being closer to the communities that they serve, with elected officials directly accountable to their constituencies. Given this, it seems logical to entrust urban governments, led by the mayors in city corporations and the heads of the municipalities, with the responsibility of providing for the primary health care needs of their populations. This function could extend to primary and secondary prevention of noncommunicable diseases.

Given the current gaps in urban governments' capacity to undertake this function, it is important that they receive adequate technical guidance and support from MOHFW, financial and administrative support from MOLGRD&C, and collaboration on multisectoral health and nutrition action across the relevant ministries. The joint participation of urban governments and MOHFW (which is responsible for secondary and tertiary health services) in the delivery of health services in urban areas would also help to strengthen referral systems. Furthermore, multisectoral action directed at health may well be easier at the urban government level, where all the relevant sectors come together.

The lessons learned from urban health capacity-building projects funded by international donors would be a good starting point to assess the capabilities and constraints of urban governments in leading on primary health service delivery. Although the experience of Chittagong (as detailed in chapter 4) is unique in

Table 6.1 Summary of Key Issues and Policy Recommendations for Urban Health Service Delivery in Bangladesh

Key issues and challenges	Policy recommendations	Key actors
Stewardship and governance Two important challenges are (a) the lack of meaningful coordination between MOHFW and MOLGRD&C on the provision of technical leadership of urban health service delivery; and (b) the inability of the urban health system to keep pace with the rapid urbanization.	*Strategy: Establishing an institutional structure for the delivery of urban health services by putting urban governments at the center of urban primary health service delivery; ensuring adequate human resources for health capacities; providing clarity on the relative roles and responsibilities of the different actors; and improving the coordination among these entities at both national and local levels, building on existing models or creating new ones* Such action would strengthen the accountability of the system by assigning more responsibility for service delivery to those responsible for implementation and closer to communities. Coordination efforts should also include the international donors that support urban health projects in Bangladesh. Specifically, this might entail the following: • Exploring coordination mechanisms at local level, whereby mayors—who are more directly accountable to the citizens—can take ownership, with support from the central level to strengthen the local capacity for coordination, planning, and oversight through appropriately trained staff and finances. • Bringing cohesion between MOHFW, MOLGRD&C, other ministries offering tertiary level health services, and the NGO and private sector by agreeing on an unambiguous division of responsibility among all the actors, aligning financial resources and accountability, and building further capacity. This process could be furthered by building on the existing urban health coordination committee established by the government. Such interministerial collaboration should also be used to further multisectoral action, for example, by improving mother's education and the design and implementation of other nutrition-sensitive programs that have a bearing on health and nutrition outcomes. • Aligning all international donors' support for urban health—including those related to service delivery, reporting and quality control, mapping of facilities to certain catchment areas, and enlisting of the poor with periodic updates—with the government of Bangladesh's National Urban Health Strategy.	*Leading roles:* Ministry of Planning; MOHFW; MOLGRD&C (LGD); urban governments *Supporting roles:* Other ministries providing urban services; international donors for technical support and financial assistance, as required

table continues next page

Table 6.1 Summary of Key Issues and Policy Recommendations for Urban Health Service Delivery in Bangladesh *(continued)*

Key issues and challenges	Policy recommendations	Key actors
Regulation Regulation appears weak and outdated, and the implementation of existing policies and regulations is a key bottleneck. There are provisions for quality control, but these are not effectively enforced and are often purely an administrative exercise. Similarly, the Medical Practice, Private Clinics and Laboratories Ordinance dates back to 1982 and is also not fully enforced.	*Strategy: Strengthening the regulatory structures and processes for urban health services delivery* Selective new regulations will need to be formulated, and both new and existing regulations will need to be enforced adequately and consistently. The regulatory measures must be accompanied by the establishment of viable clinical quality assurance mechanisms as well as periodic audits by MOHFW to monitor compliance of providers with standards, in collaboration with the relevant professional associations. Such measures would include the following: • Revising and updating regulations on licensing and registration and ensuring that quality controls are conducted periodically to monitor adequacy of infrastructure, human resources, and adherence to standards and protocols (at least for those services listed in the essential service package), with appropriate follow-up on filling identified gaps. • Making Hospital Management Committees a mandatory part of the hospital and health facilities management structure, including ensuring effective representation from civil society and engaging them actively in addressing the challenges of hospitals and suggesting changes. • Encouraging the professional associations to play a bigger role in promoting a stronger patient-centered culture among providers.	*Leading roles:* MOHFW; MOLGRD&C
Financing There is no fiscal decentralization for urban health sector, and no local participation in the resource allocation function. The de jure focus on expanding the responsibilities of urban governments for health service delivery has not been accompanied by separate line item budgets for health.	*Strategy: Ensuring sustainable financing for urban health and for urban governments to deliver urban health services* Potential options to achieve this might include the following: • Aligning financing with responsibilities for urban health by ensuring adequate financing targeted at the delivery and coordination of the planned health services from the central-level budget (as urban governments play a more active role in planning for urban health services in their areas), and exploring options to complement those funds with revenues collected at the local level (as in the Chittagong City Corporation), while being mindful of the centralized processes in place in Bangladesh. • Updating and standardizing user fees for essential services and/or for the most common procedures.	*Leading roles:* Ministry of Finance (Finance Division); Ministry of Planning; MOHFW; MOLGRD&C *Supporting roles:* Academic institutions; NGOs; international donors for technical support and financial assistance, as necessary

table continues next page

table continues next page

Table 6.1 Summary of Key Issues and Policy Recommendations for Urban Health Service Delivery in Bangladesh (continued)

Key issues and challenges	Policy recommendations	Key actors
	• Standardizing the methods used to identify the poor and the levels of exemption from user fees, and ensuring the full compliance of providers with these exemptions. • Exploring the use of cash transfers to induce behavioral change in urban areas of Bangladesh (especially for reducing stunting, which is a critical development challenge and where other countries have had success in the use of such transfers). This is an area in which the World Bank, given its rich experience with cash transfer programs around the world, might be able to assist Bangladesh.	
Service delivery The delivery of urban health services by the public is insufficient to satisfy the demand and need for such services. There is no planning at the local government level to avoid duplication of services and to ensure that these offer a comprehensive range of services. The referral system is dysfunctional. The public and private sector, including the NGOs, have been especially successful in promoting family planning, infectious disease prevention, and diarrheal treatment, but less successful in the areas of maternal and child undernutrition—a critical need in urban areas.	*Strategy: Establishing a people-centered integrated care health system and fostering public-private collaboration in the delivery of urban health services* As a way of reducing the fragmentation of the delivery system, it would be important to shift the model from an approach that targets specific groups of the population to one that addresses the needs of the entire population and moves toward a culture of patient-centeredness. Steps that could be taken in this regard include the following: • Making sure that providers are offering services that cater to the needs of the entire population. There is a need for iterative learning from testing interventions for improving the quality and increasing the use of health services—whether the service provider is public, NGO, or private—by the urban poor and slum residents. The scope of interventions needs to move beyond maternal and child health services to respond to the epidemic of noncommunicable diseases as well as to reach underserved groups, including working males. • Making services more accessible to the working population by expanding the hours of operations to early morning and late evening both at the facilities and at outreach services and clinics in slum settlements. • Actively pursuing the current plans for establishing a functioning referral system by ensuring proper population empanelment, especially for the permanent population, and exploring mechanisms by which all facilities, including the private ones, are committed to providing services to the identified population in a catchment area. This should become a key responsibility of urban governments. • Working with the professional associations to promote a culture of patient-centeredness, quality, and accountability among providers.	*Leading roles:* MOHFW; MOLGRD&C *Supporting roles:* Public and private sector service providers; academic institutions; NGOs; international donors for technical support and financial assistance, as necessary

table continues next page

Table 6.1 Summary of Key Issues and Policy Recommendations for Urban Health Service Delivery in Bangladesh *(continued)*

Key issues and challenges	Policy recommendations	Key actors
	• Considering the feasibility of implementing interventions—such as social marketing, vouchers, franchising, regulation, accreditation, and contracting—that have been tested in various low- and middle-income country settings to improve the utilization and quality of private RMNCH services. The government should carefully explore and test options—in areas such as financing, insurance, service delivery contracting, regulation, and accreditation—that may improve the quality of care provided by the private sector (while minimizing any negative effects on the viability of private providers). Such efforts should be accompanied by rigorous formative and evaluative research. • Ensuring that patients arriving at the secondary- or tertiary-level facility with referrals from lower levels receive timely treatment, as opposed to those who do not have referrals, to change the perception that referrals are merely suggestions. • Ensuring that facilities have anonymous mechanisms to report staff behavior to management and that sanctions are enforced on staff who do not treat patients with respect. This would include identifying and enforcing effective ways of receiving and addressing complaints through dialogue with representatives of the local communities. • Requiring regular reporting to the central level (not only to international donors) on overall performance, including quality of care. • Given that the private sector (for-profit and nonprofit) is the main provider of health services in urban areas, including to the poor, effective partnerships are necessary to help ensure private-provider quality of care. The government should carefully explore and test options—in areas such as financing, insurance, service delivery contracting, regulation, and accreditation—that would facilitate collaboration and improve the quality of care in the private health sector. The involvement in this process of the pharmacies and pharmacists, who are integral to urban health service delivery, is critical.	

table continues next page

Table 6.1 Summary of Key Issues and Policy Recommendations for Urban Health Service Delivery in Bangladesh *(continued)*

Key issues and challenges	Policy recommendations	Key actors
Monitoring and evaluation The monitoring and evaluation function is not coordinated at the central level. The National Health Management Information System (HMIS), residing within MOHFW, covers all MOHFW facilities in rural and urban areas, but it does not capture data from the other government facilities, NGOs, and the for-profit private sector. There is no mechanism for feeding data back to the lower levels and to facilities for on-course corrections.	*Strategy: Building a comprehensive M&E system to facilitate effective monitoring of public and private urban health services and programs as well as evidence-based decision making* This system would entail consistent and comprehensive reporting and monitoring of all conditions through the HMIS, so that the national HMIS covers not only the rural areas and the secondary and tertiary facilities under MOHFW but also all primary health facilities in urban areas, including NGO-run and the private for-profit facilities. The M&E efforts can be strengthened considerably by leveraging existing technology, specifically as follows: • Bangladesh has already established a national HMIS, which collects data from rural areas and from secondary and tertiary facilities in urban areas. It would be important to consolidate information on urban primary health care through this system, so that information can flow to the central level and be fed back to the lower levels and the facilities. • There are some promising initiatives for collecting more data more consistently from the various urban primary health facilities, and scaling up existing efforts of common reporting of all facilities through the rollout of the DHS2 survey (UHSSP pilot); it would be worthwhile to consider building on such experiences. • The routine monitoring should be buttressed by strategic use of operations research as well as periodic survey-based project and program evaluations to guide policy making.	*Leading role:* MOHFW *Supporting roles:* MOLGRD&C (LGD); urban governments; NGOs and private providers; international donors
Voice and accountability The culture of accountability within the health system is weak, and there is no clarity on patients' rights. There is a limited sense of trust established between the provider and the patients, and the relationship is hierarchical.	*Strategy: Strengthening accountability in the delivery of urban health services* This could be undertaken through measures such as the following: • Encouraging the health departments of urban governments to work with the existing channels of community representation to strengthen citizens' understanding of health promotion, prevention, and citizens' rights vis-à-vis the health system, including information on service offerings, types of formal or registered facilities available in the area, hours of operation, risks and hidden costs of delaying medical care, and so on. • Increasing citizens' voice by exploring more effective ways to organize their representation to ensure the voices of different groups are expressed (for example, women's groups and appropriate representation on the Hospital Management Committee). • Establishing, over time, a more regular patient-provider relationship through population empanelment and enforcement of (some level of) gatekeeping.	*Leading roles:* Urban governments; NGOs focusing on human rights; professional associations; public and private sector health providers

table continues next page

Table 6.1 Summary of Key Issues and Policy Recommendations for Urban Health Service Delivery in Bangladesh *(continued)*

Key issues and challenges	Policy recommendations	Key actors
Urban and urban health policy Urbanization and the urban health milieu in Bangladesh have evolved rapidly, without a concurrent emergence of a vision of how the urban health system should work.	*Strategy: Developing a shared urban health policy, within the broader context of urbanization and urban policy, with a strong focus on the needs of slum residents* Such a policy would entail the following: • Underlining a stronger stewardship role for the government, reflecting better the evolving operating environment, including increasingly relevant issues such as rural-urban migration; the changing epidemiological and demographic profiles of urban areas; the rapid development of slum settlements; the potential for multisectoral action to influence health and nutrition indicators; the unique urban governance structures; the needs of a working population; and the health human resource, financing, and service provision realities on the ground. • Effectively addressing maternal and child undernutrition in urban (slum) areas, especially focusing on two higher level actions: (a) higher political and bureaucratic prioritization of nutrition in the country's health development agenda in particular, and its economic development agenda more generally; and (b) a more central treatment of maternal and child nutrition for the urban poor and slum residents in the development and implementation of government national health strategies and operational plans, including in the strategies and plans related to urban health. This would require the government to also adjust its policy stance regarding slum settlements to one that actively promotes the interests and welfare of slum residents and treats slum residents as a primary target group in the country's development agenda.	*Leading roles:* Prime Minister's Office; Ministry of Planning; MOHFW; MOLGRD&C *Supporting roles:* Other ministries; international donors to support with experiences from other countries

Note: DHS2 = Demographic and Health Survey 2014; HMIS = Health Management Information System; LGD = Local Government Division; M&E = monitoring and evaluation; MOHFW = Ministry of Health and Family Welfare; MOLGRD&C = Ministry of Local Government, Rural Development, and Co-operatives; NGO = nongovernmental organization; RMNCH = reproductive, maternal, newborn, and child health; UHSSP = Urban Health Systems Strengthening Project.

Bangladesh given the city's history and relative affluence, certain aspects of the "Chittagong model" (such as the ownership and leadership of the city corporation in taking responsibility for health) could be leveraged by other urban governments for the development of effective primary health services.

Ensuring Sustainable Financing for Urban Governments

For urban governments to effectively implement health programs, it is vital that they receive adequate and reliable financing. By the same token, it is important that urban governments be held accountable for the effective use of provided funds. In many other LMICs, urban governments have the authority and ability to independently raise revenues for delivering health services. It may be worthwhile to explore the possibly of such revenue generation, at least by city corporations in Bangladesh.

In addition, it is conceivable that a portion of the block grants provided by MOLGRD&C to urban governments could be earmarked for the delivery of health services. Such earmarking should be accompanied by effective accountability systems so that the urban governments' use of funds for the delivery of health services can be monitored and assessed.

Building Human Resources for Health Capacities in Urban Governments

It is important to ensure that the cadres of health professionals and paraprofessionals have a clear career path within urban governments. An option is to hire these cadres using the same systems that MOHFW uses, so that professionals can move seamlessly between MOHFW and urban government structures. Such a recruitment system should be accompanied by effective capacity building and a system of continuing education.

Fostering Public-Private Partnerships in Urban Health Service Delivery

The private sector is the main provider of health services in urban Bangladesh, including to the poor. Although urban governments contract with NGOs to provide health services, the available evidence often suggests modest or no effects on health outcomes of interest, even if NGO health service utilization increases. Urban governments should extend their role beyond regulation, and consider actively partnering with the private sector as well. This would include experimenting with alternative approaches, focused on extending the scope of the private sector into preventive and promotive health services as well as ensuring a minimum level of service quality that is affordable to the poor.

Given that pharmacies are so ubiquitous and hence such critical entities in urban health service delivery, the government should make efforts to engage them in this dialogue and to foster an active collaboration that entails a combination of pharmacy accreditation and pharmacist training and continuing education in partnership with their professional association. Contracting arrangements with NGOs should also be adapted to go beyond coverage and utilization to service quality considerations. As noted earlier, these partnerships with NGOs and private health providers should also go beyond the provision of RMNCH services to the prevention and treatment of noncommunicable diseases, given the already high and rapidly rising contribution of noncommunicable diseases to death and disability in urban areas.

Building a Comprehensive Monitoring and Evaluation System for Effective Monitoring of Urban Health Programs and Evidence-Based Decision Making

Instituting an urban health sector management information system (MIS) that provides reliable and regular information, and ready access to statistics by decision makers, is a priority. The potential value of the health sector MIS would increase to the extent that it (a) covers not only public health facilities but also NGO and private health providers, and (b) can collect data on quality-of-care indicators. The MIS should cover city corporations, municipalities, and other urban areas—ideally also being integrated with other sources of administrative and survey data on public environmental conditions and services gathered by relevant urban government units, ministries, and the Bangladesh Bureau of Statistics.

Putting Slums at the Center of Urban (Including Urban Health) Policy

Developing clear, sound policies on the treatment of slum settlements—and on the provision of public environmental and health services in slum settlements—is an imperative. Given that urban areas face multiple health risks arising from poor environmental conditions and services (with amplified risks in slum settlements and other poor neighborhoods), policies and regulations should span health-sensitive ministries such as water resources, social welfare, food and disaster management, education, fisheries and livestock, industries, and the environment.

Fortunately, efforts are currently under way in Bangladesh to formulate an urban health policy and operational plan. These sector-level efforts should be accompanied by an effort to introduce supportive policies and regulations addressing the urgent needs of the proliferating slum settlements in a rapidly urbanizing Bangladesh.

References

Alam, Mahbub-Ul, Farzana Yeasmin, Farzana Begum, Mahbubur Rahman, Fosiul Alam Nisame, Stephen Luby, Peter Winch, and Leanne Unicomb. 2016. "Can Behaviour Change Approaches Improve the Cleanliness and Functionality of Shared Toilets? A Randomized Control Trial in Dhaka, Bangladesh." Discussion Paper No. 9, Water & Sanitation for the Urban Poor (WSUP), London.

Alderman, Harold, and Derek D. Headey. 2017. "How Important Is Parental Education for Child Nutrition?" World Development 94: 448–64.

Bennett, Daniel, and Wesley Yin. 2014. "The Market for High-Quality Medicine." Working Paper No. 20091, National Bureau of Economic Research (NBER), Cambridge, MA.

Björkman-Nyqvist, Martina, Jakob Svensson, and David Yanagizawa-Drott. 2012. "Can Good Products Drive Out Bad? Evidence from Local Markets for (Fake?)

AntiMalarial Medicine in Uganda." Discussion Paper 9114, Center for Economic Policy Research, London.

Das, Jishnu, Alaka Holla, Aakash Mohpal, and Karthik Muralidharan. 2016. "Quality and Accountability in Health Care Delivery: Audit-Study Evidence from Primary Care in India." *American Economic Review* 106 (12): 3765–99.

El Arifeen, Shams, Aliki Christou, Laura Reichenbach, Ferdous Arfina Osman, Kishwar Azad, Khaled Shamsul Islam, Faruque Ahmed, Henry B. Perry, and David H. Peters. 2013. "Community-Based Approaches and Partnerships: Innovations in Health-Service Delivery in Bangladesh." *Lancet* 382 (9909): 2012–26.

Fakir, Adnan M. S., and M. Wasiqur Rahman Khan. 2015. "Determinants of Malnutrition among Urban Slum Children in Bangladesh." *Health Economics Review* 5 (1): 1–11.

Goudet, Sophie, Paula Griffiths, Barry Bogin, and Nyovani Madise. 2017. "Interventions to Tackle Malnutrition and Its Risk Factors in Children Living in Slums: A Scoping Review." *Annals of Human Biology* 44 (1): 1–10.

Madhavan S., D. Bishai, C. Stanton, and A. Harding. 2010. "Engaging the Private Sector in Maternal and Neonatal Health in Low and Middle Income Countries." Working Paper 12, Future Health Systems Research Programme Consortium, Johns Hopkins University, Baltimore.

Manley, James, Seth Gitter, and Vanya Slavchevska. 2013. "How Effective Are Cash Transfers at Improving Nutritional Status?" *World Development* 48 (C): 133–55.

NIPORT (National Institute of Population Research and Training), Mitra and Associates, and ICF International. 2016. "Bangladesh Demographic and Health Survey 2014." Dhaka, Bangladesh; Rockville, MD: NIPORT, Mitra and Associates, and ICF International,

Patouillard, Edith, Catherine A. Goodman, Kara G. Hanson, and Anne J. Mills. 2007. "Can Working with the Private For-Profit Sector Improve Utilization of Quality Health Services by the Poor? A Systematic Review of the Literature." *International Journal for Equity in Health* 6: 17.

Peal, Andy, Barbara Evans, Isabel Blackett, Peter Hawkins, and Chris Heymans. 2014. "Fecal Sludge Management: A Comparative Analysis of 12 Cities." *Journal of Water, Sanitation and Hygiene for Development* 4 (4): 563–75.

Ross, Ian, Rebecca Scott, and Ravikumar Joseph. 2016. "Fecal Sludge Management: Diagnostics for Service Delivery in Urban Areas." Water and Sanitation Program (WSP) Technical Paper, Working Paper No. 106805, World Bank, Washington, DC.

Ruel, Marie T., Harold Alderman, and the Maternal and Child Nutrition Study Group. 2013. "Nutrition-Sensitive Interventions and Programmes: How Can They Help to Accelerate Progress in Improving Maternal and Child Nutrition?" *Lancet* 382 (9891): 536–51.

World Bank. 2003. "Decentralization of Health Care in Brazil: A Case Study of Bahia." Report No. 24416-BR, World Bank, Washington, DC.

* 9 7 8 1 4 6 4 8 1 1 9 9 9 *